T0401075

LITERACY AND THE INCLUSIVE CLASSROOM

EDUCATION IN A COMPETITIVE AND GLOBALIZING WORLD

Additional books in this series can be found on Nova's website under the Series tab.

Additional E-books in this series can be found on Nova's website under the E-book tab.

EDUCATION IN A COMPETITIVE AND GLOBALIZING WORLD

LITERACY AND THE INCLUSIVE CLASSROOM

SANDRA L. FERRARA

Nova Science Publishers, Inc.
New York

For permission to use material from this book please contact us:
Telephone 631-231-7269; Fax 631-231-8175
Web Site: http://www.novapublishers.com

NOTICE TO THE READER

The Publisher has taken reasonable care in the preparation of this book, but makes no expressed or implied warranty of any kind and assumes no responsibility for any errors or omissions. No liability is assumed for incidental or consequential damages in connection with or arising out of information contained in this book. The Publisher shall not be liable for any special, consequential, or exemplary damages resulting, in whole or in part, from the readers' use of, or reliance upon, this material. Any parts of this book based on government reports are so indicated and copyright is claimed for those parts to the extent applicable to compilations of such works.

Independent verification should be sought for any data, advice or recommendations contained in this book. In addition, no responsibility is assumed by the publisher for any injury and/or damage to persons or property arising from any methods, products, instructions, ideas or otherwise contained in this publication.

This publication is designed to provide accurate and authoritative information with regard to the subject matter covered herein. It is sold with the clear understanding that the Publisher is not engaged in rendering legal or any other professional services. If legal or any other expert assistance is required, the services of a competent person should be sought. FROM A DECLARATION OF PARTICIPANTS JOINTLY ADOPTED BY A COMMITTEE OF THE AMERICAN BAR ASSOCIATION AND A COMMITTEE OF PUBLISHERS.

Additional color graphics may be available in the e-book version of this book.

LIBRARY OF CONGRESS CATALOGING-IN-PUBLICATION DATA

Ferrara, Sandra L.
  Literacy and the inclusive classroom / Sandra L. Ferrara.
      p. cm.
  Includes bibliographical references and index.
  ISBN 978-1-61324-659-7 (hardcover)
  1. Reading (Elementary) 2. Literacy. 3. Inclusive education. I. Title.
  LB1573.F43 2011
  372.4--dc22
                        2011015620

Published by Nova Science Publishers, Inc. † New York

This book is dedicated to Bradley, Michael, and Craigen, my incredible sons. You are my inspiration for all time.

CONTENTS

PREFACE

Literacy, the ability to read and write proficiently, is essential in almost every facet of modern life. Alarmingly, a staggering number of U.S. children are functioning below acceptable literacy levels. What can be done to remedy this situation? Teachers need the knowledge and skills to reach all children. This book covers the essentials of literacy learning and teaching in the early grades. The material is presented in a straight forward way and is intended for pre-service educators and new educators working in inclusive settings. Teachers working in inclusive classrooms face unique challenges. In this new book literacy development is examined from multiple perspectives, and it includes information regarding language development, characteristics of students with special needs, phonological awareness, the alphabetic principle, word recognition, vocabulary, fluency, comprehension, written expression, assessment, and instructional strategies.

Sandra Ferrara, Ed.D.
The College of Saint Rose
Albany, New York 12203

Chapter 1

INTRODUCTION

A room without books is like a body without a soul.
(Cicero, Roman author, 106 BC – 43 BC)

Literacy, the ability to read and write proficiently, is essential in almost all facets of modern life. Certainly, literacy skills are indispensable in reading a book for information or pleasure and filling out a job application, but literacy skills are also important in other undeniable ways. From sending and receiving text messages to understanding a bank statement and paying monthly bills, literacy skills are vital to a child's future independence and quality of life. Teachers, in concert with the support of families and communities, can give children the gift of a literate life—a gift that will last a lifetime. Today there is a great need to move beyond mere good intentions, because good intentions alone are often not enough to insure that all children will develop the skills necessary for a truly literate life.

The goal of this book is to look at important research findings, explore what is known about literacy learning and teaching, take into consideration child development, characteristics of children with special needs, and combine this information into everyday useful suggestions for new teachers. Every page of this book is dedicated to the belief that all children can learn and indeed deserve quality instruction from exemplary teachers.

Despite recent efforts to improve reading levels over the past few years, tests demonstrate that there are far too many children who are not achieving at a basic level. Although the percentage of 4th-graders performing at or above the basic achievement level on the reading assessment portion of the National Assessment of Educational Progress (NAEP, 2007) was higher in 2007 than in 1992 (67 vs. 62 percent), this still means that 33% of 4th-graders performed below the basic achievement level. The achievement levels define what students should know and be able to do and are indicated by the following: *Basic* indicates partial mastery of fundamental skills; *Proficient* indicates demonstrated competency over challenging subject matter; and *Advanced* indicates superior performance. According to The National Center for Education Statistics, the total enrollment for fall 2007, in U.S. public and private elementary and secondary schools (pre-kindergarten through grade 12), was 55.2 million. Considering these numbers, this means a staggering number of U.S. children are functioning below acceptable literacy levels. What can be done to remedy this situation? One way to examine the problem is to begin with the scientific evidence on early literacy development.

The National Early Literacy Panel (NELP) (2008) reviewed, analyzed and summarized the research literature to find those early literacy skills that were predictive of later literacy development and instructional practices for young children that positively influenced later literacy development. The panel found six early literacy skills that consistently correlated with later literacy measures and an additional five early literacy skills that suggested importance to later literacy outcomes. Although the panel's findings point to the need for additional research studies to answer many remaining questions, the findings are still invaluable to those trying to help young children develop essential literacy skills.

Not only do educators play an important role in the development of young children's literacy skills, parents also play a vital role. Parents are their child's first and arguably their most important teachers. There are many simple ways parents can give children a good start in developing critical early literacy skills. Later, when children enter school, by continuing to participate in literacy activities at home, parents can supplement and support the school's reading program, and therefore, increase the likelihood that children will become efficient and successful readers. In the same way that a strong foundation is necessary for any successful architectural endeavor (sky scrapers, schools, museums, sports arenas, etc.), a strong foundation is essential to building the literacy skills necessary for a literate life.

The process of learning to read and write is similar to learning any new skill, whether it be a physical skill or cognitive skill. Take, for example, the process of learning to walk. First, there are prerequisite skills and abilities that are necessary. The child needs to have the physical strength to stand upright. Then the child needs the motor control to put one foot in front of the other, as well as the balance to shift body weight and remain upright. Additionally, children need motivation to keep trying when they fail (sincere encouragement from parents and siblings is helpful), and finally they need many opportunities to practice their developing skills to truly become walkers. They are not expert walkers, graceful or even efficient at first. They try and try again—one step at a time—and after many tries (successful and not so successful) the child can walk.

The same can be said of the process of learning to read and write. First, there are essential prerequisite cognitive skills. In addition, there is the need for motivation (including encouragement from parents), and finally there is the need for lots and lots of practice. Of course the process of learning to read and write is a much more mentally complicated process. However, it is not magic. There are underlying skills that build upon one another to create the strong foundation. This book presents the process of literacy skill development in children who are successful readers and examines the issues and challenges applicable to children with disabilities.

Laying the foundation early is extremely important. Research in the field of reading demonstrates that young children who develop efficient early reading skills are more likely to have successful learning experiences in their school careers (National Reading Panel, 2000). Furthermore, The National Early Literacy Panel (2008) more recently reported that there are many skills and abilities of young children (birth through five years) that are predictive of later literacy skills. Table 1.1 highlights the important predictors.

Table 1.1 Predictive Early Literacy Skills

Phonological awareness: The ability to recognize, manipulate, or analyze the parts of spoken language (words, syllables, phonemes)
Phonological memory: The ability to remember auditory information (short term)
Rapid automatic naming of letters or digits (ability to rapidly name a sequence of random letters or digits)
Rapid automatic naming of objects or colors (rapidly name sets of pictures or colors)
Writing letters or name (ability to write letters in isolation or to write one's own name) Alphabet knowledge: Letter--sound correspondence (knows names and sounds of printed letters)

In addition, the NELP (2008) report suggested the following as other important abilities of young children (0—5 yrs.): Oral language, reading readiness, prior knowledge, concepts about print, and visual processing. Moreover, to fully understand the all important foundational skills for all children, it is important to examine the most effective ways to help children who are at-risk for reading failure. According to Suggate (2010), a developmental understanding of reading remediation is vitally important since age and experience play roles in these foundational abilities. Furthermore, a synthesis of research suggests that phonics interventions are more effective with younger children, while comprehension and mixed interventions are more effective thereafter (Suggate, 2010).

Together, all these underlying skills lay the foundation for efficient literacy skill development. Teachers need to be mindful of the foundation they are helping to build, including why and how each part of literacy development is related to the others. Each of these essential literacy skills will be discussed in the chapters that follow.

QUESTIONS FOR REFLECTION AND DISCUSSION

1) Think back to your early school experiences. What memories do you have of learning to read? Are these memories positive? Explain why or why not.
2) Do you remember leaning how to "decode" words? If so, what do you remember?
3) Was reading instruction provided in small groups, whole class, or both?
4) What do you remember about being read to as a child, either at home, or in school? What were your favorite children's books? How did they capture and keep your attention?
5) What are your earliest memories of writing?
6) How will you set up your classroom and plan instruction to promote positive attitudes toward literacy for all of your students?
7) Do you remember any children with special needs in your primary grade classrooms? If so, what do you remember about how they were included?

CHAPTER APPLICATION EXERCISES

1) Interview a primary level teacher about his or her experiences teaching literacy. Find out about the classroom environment, the amount of time for literacy instruction, how he or she balances instruction of the various components of literacy, and how the needs of the learners in the class are met. Summarize your findings in a one page paper.
2) Find a peer reviewed published study of early literacy skills. Write an article critique, and include the following: 1) summarize the study and results; 2) critique the study (your opinion of the strengths and limitations of the study); 3) describe how the results translate to classroom instruction.

Chapter 2

KEY IDEAS IN LITERACY DEVELOPMENT

"Every successive generation becomes a living memorial of our public
schools, and a living example of their existence."
(Joseph Story, U.S. Supreme Court Justice)

THE HEART OF A TEACHER

What does it take to be a good teacher, an effective teacher, a teacher that
makes a difference? What does it mean to have the heart of a teacher? This
chapter addresses the characteristics and qualities that research suggests effective
teachers possess, the techniques they use, and how they organize and manage their
classrooms.

One of the most important factors in children's literacy development is the
teacher (Moats, 1999). Therefore, it is essential that pre-service and beginning
teachers not only develop the knowledge base and skills that are critical to
teaching literacy skills to young children, but they also need to have opportunities
to apply that knowledge in real classroom settings under the guidance of expert
teachers. The breadth and depth of the required literacy knowledge and skills that
go into making an expert teacher are considerable, and there is much to learn from
examining what expert teachers do and how they do it. In order to become a
highly effective literacy teacher, a teacher must confidently know: The essential
skills that comprise reading and writing and how to teach those skills; the most
appropriate sequence for the introduction of skills and concepts; how to examine
and select reading programs to meet all children's needs; effective lesson planning
and implementation; techniques for assessing, monitoring progress, correcting

errors, and making adjustments to instruction as needed; and how to motivate children and maximize the time children spend engaged in reading (Carnine, Silbert, Kame'enui, & Tarver, 2010).

The heart of a teacher is a term used here to include all the attitudes and beliefs, as well as all the knowledge and skills that go into making someone an exemplary teacher. Teaching children to read and write is a noble endeavor. As such, the role of teacher is one to be honored and respected. Although often underestimated, in reality the responsibilities to individual children, their families, and society are enormous. Having the heart of a teacher means that priorities for learning, expectations for success, the value each child brings to the setting, and the belief that all children can learn are considerations that are always in focus. Effective teachers are purposeful, flexible, and tenacious. In addition, having the heart of a teacher means understanding that the relationship between child and teacher is very important. In fact without the development of rapport between teacher and child, learning may be compromised (Lerner, 2003). Having the heart of a teacher means believing that children can and will learn and carrying out instruction accordingly (Pressley, Allington, Wharton-McDonald, Block, & Morrow, 2001). In addition to having high expectations and being superior motivators, Gunning (2010) suggests highly effective teachers have the following qualities: Highly effective teachers are quick to respond to student instructional needs; they reinforce skills and make connections; they use scaffolding to support student learning; they have established classroom routines that promote student responsibility and a sense of purpose and order within an atmosphere of cooperation; they use high quality materials and make them available for various kinds of reading; they challenge students (and give support as needed) based on progress monitoring information; they keep up with developments in the field; and highly effective teachers reflect on their teaching in terms of student outcomes.

When teachers create a classroom environment and atmosphere that communicate an enthusiasm for literacy, the enthusiasm can become contagious and motivational. Teachers who are avid readers and spread their love of reading to their students through sharing, discussing, and reading to them every day, are creating the ideal conditions for students to develop their own enthusiasm and motivation for reading.

In a comparison of effective and less-effective teachers in low-income schools, researchers found that the effective teachers provided more of the following in their classrooms: Small-group instruction; scaffolding and support; phonics instruction and practice in connected text; in-depth questions (inferences, etc.); wide independent reading; time engaged in reading and writing activities;

and outreach and involvement of parents (Taylor, Pearson, Clark, & Walpole, 2000). Furthermore, expert teachers have developed the capacity to make accurate and efficient inferences, differentiate relevant from irrelevant information, and have an awareness of and comprehension of the activities within their classrooms (McCown, Driscoll, Roop, 1996). In other words, effective teachers have a handle on their classrooms and can sift through the complex nature of a dynamic classroom to adjust learning situations and address the needs of their students.

Likewise, to have the heart of a teacher means to have the heart of a learner. Effective teachers are life-long learners who continually learn from the children they teach, from other teachers and peers, and from the field of literacy education and educational research. Teaching and learning can be viewed as aspects of the same process or cycle, and as mentioned previously, a teacher's view of learning and teaching influences his or her instructional planning and practice.

The findings of the National Reading Panel (2000) point to the importance of systematic and explicit instruction in the areas of phonemic awareness, alphabetic knowledge and phonics, fluency, vocabulary, and comprehension. This requires that teachers have a firm foundation (knowledge and experience with application) in all of these areas so that instruction is clear, modeling is used effectively, children are provided with many opportunities to practice and review, and teachers and children interact together to promote the best possible outcomes in literacy development. When teachers create an efficient and effective learning environment that increases learner competence, they are also creating a humane environment that enhances a child's self-concept (Carnine, et al., 2010). In addition, when teachers make literacy learning fun and exciting, and they align instructional objectives with instruction that guides and systematically supports children in reaching their goals, children benefit. It makes sense that children who are fortunate enough to have exciting and skillful teachers become motivated to read and write even more.

Increasingly, motivation is an issue that has to be addressed. For whatever reason, (perhaps a lack of success in the past, or something else that may not be readily apparent) a child may not be motivated to put forth enough effort or may appear to give up easily. In this case, it is imperative that teachers take the time to help all children develop a positive interest in learning to read and write. One of the first steps is to make sure each child has an opportunity to experience success through the use of carefully designed and effectively presented lessons that are followed by high levels of positive reinforcement (Carnine, et al., 2010). However, Becker, McElvany, and Kortenbruck (2010) conducted a longitudinal study regarding reading and motivation and offer the following words of caution,

... the problem is thus not always that students fail to learn because they lack motivation; rather, students lack motivation because they do not experience progress and competence. The present findings indicate that this holds even for the very young students analyzed here. In order to motivate students, teachers must therefore offer them the experience of progress and competence. Additionally, the negative effects of extrinsic motivation on later reading literacy have clear implications for teachers and parents. Student reading motivated by the wish to please parents or teachers does not promote achievement gains over time. (p. 782).

Similarly, Archambault, Eccles, and Vida (2010) recommend that teachers provide specific interventions to promote intrinsic motivation and opportunities for success, especially for children who demonstrate motivational declines early (the first two years), in order to catch them while they still feel good about their abilities and think reading and writing are important skills. One of the best ways to promote intrinsic motivation in literacy activities is to find out what interests and excites a particular child, and then provide appropriate level materials that involve those specified interests.

Furthermore, there are several essential procedures effective literacy teachers use to assure they address the needs of all children. First of all, assessments are used to identify needs and address any problem areas early so that the focus is more on prevention in the immediate term rather than on remediation later. Next, progress is continually monitored to determine the effectiveness of instruction in general or an intervention in particular, and then changes and adjustments in instruction are made according to the needs of individual children. In this way the selected literacy interventions, including planning and instruction, are a deliberate attempt to build the foundational skills that have been associated with later facility in reading and writing.

Similar in nature to what individual teachers do to address the needs of all children, there is a recent system-wide model of instruction that integrates these prevention practices, with scientific research evidence and educational policy. In the past several years an evidence-based general education initiative, known as Response to Intervention (RTI) has been introduced as a prevention model in public schools. RTI features multiple tiers of interventions (in this case reading) that are meant to support early literacy skill development. Within the RTI model there is a "continuum of increasingly intensive, specialized instruction" introduced early in a child's school experiences (National Research Center on Learning Disabilities, 2003, p. 3). More information will be presented in later chapters.

Many people refer to teaching as a calling. Teaching is not for the faint hearted, nor the unprepared. There are struggles to be sure and the responsibility is huge. However, the rewards can be even greater. To witness and positively influence the intellectual, social, and emotional growth of children is an awe-inspiring occasion. In his examination of the nature of success, Malcolm Gladwell (2008, p. 11), says, "...the values of the world we inhabit and the people we surround ourselves with have a profound effect on who we are." This is a powerful idea and speaks to the tremendous influence teachers have in the direction of children's lives. Think about teachers who have a positive impact. What are their qualities? What do they do? One of the important responsibilities of each teacher is to create a classroom climate that is safe, supportive, conducive to learning, and joyful. Teachers must help foster a supportive community of learning that values all children. Gladwell goes on to say, "...no one—not rock stars, not professional athletes, not software billionaires, and not even geniuses—ever makes it alone." (2008, p. 115). Each child's life is significant, and each deserves the opportunity to blossom with the help of dedicated, knowledgeable, and passionate teachers. Michelle Rhee (2011) states, "Once inside the school, a great teacher is the single most important factor in a child's education. While there are many factors that influence a student's ability to learn, a great teacher can help any student overcome those barriers and realize their full potential." (StudentsFirst.org, Mission Statement, 2011). Students in teacher preparation programs, as well as teachers already in the field, need to consider carefully the roles and responsibilities involved in a career in education.

THEORETICAL PERSPECTIVES

Examination of the underlying theoretical perspectives of literacy instruction is important. When theory, research, and practice come together a deeper understanding is possible. With a deeper understanding of the whys, and wherefores of typical literacy development teachers will be better able to gauge the status of literacy instruction in general, as well as make specific adjustments based on evidence. That is, teachers will be empowered to make informed instructional decisions in their efforts to better serve all children. When more children reach their full potential in literacy development, society as a whole will benefit. Failure should not be an option. There is no doubt the job of teaching literacy skills to young children is an extremely important one. According to Moats (1999), reading instruction is a complex endeavor that requires expertise, in-depth knowledge, and is the most fundamental responsibility that schools have.

Theory helps shine a light on the process of literacy development, helps make sense of classroom and home observations, and helps sort out the abundance of information available, thereby informing instructional planning and practice. A sound researched-based theory may be analogous to a Global Positioning System (GPS). Sound theory as a basis for instructional assessment, planning, implementation, and progress monitoring has the capability to inform teachers of where students are (in terms of literacy development) and can direct teachers where they want to go with children's literacy development. Although the analogy is thought-provoking and makes a point, literacy development cannot be simplified to following a series of directions, "… turn right, go three miles and you have reached your destination". Just as the inter-workings of a GPS are very complex, the inter-workings of literacy development are also very complex.

Bottom-up, Top-down, and Interactive Perspectives

Literacy theories or perspectives are a way to view the process of literacy development. When theories are based on sound research evidence, they can be very helpful in guiding literacy instruction. With this in mind, new research evidence may either support or refute the principles of a theoretical perspective, thereby revising the view of the literacy development in the process. The theoretical perspectives of literacy development are often divided into three general categories; bottom-up, top-down, and interactive. The bottom-up perspective of literacy development emphasizes the text and foundational skill (sometimes called sub-skill) development and suggests that meaning is derived from the accurate and sequential processing of linguistic units (letters, words, phrases). At the other end of the spectrum, the top-down perspective on literacy development emphasizes the reader, and suggests that meaning is derived when the child uses experiences and background knowledge, including language ability, to obtain meaning. Finally, the interactive perspective is a combination of the two, and suggests that meaning is derived from the accurate processing of text, the use of background knowledge and experiences, and language ability. Similarly, reading may be viewed as a transaction between a child and a text (Rosenblatt, 2004). In this manner, the child makes use of prior knowledge to make connections with what they are reading in a dynamic and responsive way, and the purpose for reading a particular selection (e.g., information or pleasure) is highly relevant to comprehension.

Cognitive Psychology

Broader theoretical perspectives relevant to literacy development come from the work of cognitive psychology and have to do with human perception, thinking, and learning. Two theorists of note, Jean Piaget and Lev Vygotsky, provide insight into children's cognitive development, and therefore, literacy development.

First, Jean Piaget, a Swiss biologist, is well known for his stage theory of cognitive development. His four stages include: sensorimotor; preoperational; concrete-operational; and formal-operational. The first three stages are most applicable to the literacy development of young children up to third grade. Piaget observed his own children and came up with a comprehensive account of the processes children experience during development and the cognitive structures that come with development (McCown, Driscoll, & Roop, 1996). Inherent in Piaget's theory is the idea of schemes (schemata) or mental representations of concepts. In the sensorimotor stage, the infant is concerned with sensations and motor actions, and the approximate ages are from birth to two years. During the preoperations stages, approximately 2 to 7 years, the child's actions are based on child-centered thought. That is, the thought processes of children are not logical by adult standards. This stage is noted with the following characteristics: perceptual centration, which occurs when children tend to perceive a single aspect of an object or situation to the exclusion of other important features; irreversibility, which can be observed when children are unable to mentally reverse an action; and egocentrism, which is the tendency for children to assume that they are the center of everything.

Think about the characteristics of the preoperational stage and how these characteristics relate to beginning literacy development for children from approximately 2 to 7 years of age. Very young children begin to experience literacy and literature through listening to stories, observing others read and write, and playing with and exploring the tools of literacy (drawing, scribbling, turning the pages of books, make-believe activities, computer use, etc.). During this period of development, children begin to understand that spoken words can be written down on paper. They begin to understand that symbols (graphemes) represent sounds (phonemes). However, they may focus on one aspect of an object or problem to the exclusion of other features. Therefore, the idea that the letter "c" can represent two different sounds at the beginning of a word (cat or city) may be difficult to grasp at first. Similarly, irreversibility may be an issue if children are asked to go back and order events in a story. In addition, understanding the perspective of a character in a story may bring challenges if the child cannot yet take the perspective of another. That is, children in this stage are still egocentric and think about the events in a story or a character from their own limited point of view.

The next stage of Piaget's theory is the concrete-operations stage (approximately 7 to 11 years) in which schemes become more developed and organized. Children are able to mentally reverse events, and focus on more than one aspect of a problem at a time. Various factors, such as specific child characteristics, home environment, and back ground experiences, influence when children go through the stages identified by Piaget.

Influenced by Piaget, Lev Vygotsky, a Russian scientist, developed a theoretical framework of cognitive development that takes into consideration the child's socio-cultural environment. Central to Vygotsky's theory of cognitive development is the concept of the zone of proximal development (ZPD) (Vygotsky, 1978). The ZPD is based on the concept that children have an actual or independent level of cognitive development and a potential level of cognitive development, the level they may reach with guidance. Vygotsky's framework suggests that learning is a culturally shaped activity and is influenced by the social environment of the child. Based on this idea, learning cannot be understood without considering the social context. According to Vygotsky's genetic law of cultural development:

> Any function in the child's cultural development appears twice, or on two planes. First it appears on the social plane, and then on the psychological plane. First it appears between two people as an interpsychological category, and then within the child as an intrapsychological category. This is equally true with regard to voluntary attention, logical memory, the formation of concepts, and the development of volition. (Vygotsky, 1981, p. 163)

In Vygotsky's view both social interaction and the sociocultural environment serve to create and sustain a child's cognitive development. Therefore, when specifically considering the development of literacy skills, the higher level mental processes involved in the reading process are influenced by social interaction and the sociocultural environment, including culturally developed tools. Scaffolding is the term that is used to describe the support that a skilled person may provide to children to help them move through the zone of proximal development. The role of scaffolding, specifically in the development of efficient literacy skills, should not be underestimated.

In addition to the examination of theory, an examination of personal beliefs is essential. A teacher's personal beliefs, which are derived from prior experiences, upbringing, education, and so forth, are the foundation for instructional planning and implementation. Together the theoretical perspective taken and an individual teacher's personal philosophy of teaching and learning, influence everything from instructional goals, methods, materials, and classroom organization, to the evaluation of program. Therefore, a thorough exploration of personal beliefs and their relationship to theoretical perspectives of literacy development should be a part of every teacher's preparation and regular self reflection.

Memory: Storage and Retrieval

Learning in general, and learning to read and write in particular, are all considered to be mental activities. In our fast changing world of computers and technology, one way to conceptualize mental activity or mental processes is with an information-processing model or theory that includes the processes of encoding, storing, and retrieving information (McCowen, Driscoll, & Roop, 1996). Information processing theory, as a model of how memory works, can be instructive in determining the best ways to improve retention or learning, and consequently helping children develop all the foundational skills necessary for optimal literacy development. An understanding of how memory works will help teachers plan lessons and design instruction to enhance the retention of information.

In the first part of the system or stage of the information processing model the child receives information from the environment. This is part of the encoding stage. All of the senses receive information (into what is called the sensory register). The child hears the sounds of the classroom—papers shuffling, the noise of the fan, voices of children, and so on. The child also sees the activities of the classroom—the teacher moving around the room, other children writing, reading, drawing, the visual displays on the bulletin boards, the information on the board, and the Smart Board. The child also experiences the smells of the school environment—markers, glue, clay, other children, janitorial cleaning supplies, and the aromas of food cooking in the school kitchen. The child also feels the environment in terms of the materials he or she comes in contact with, as well as in terms of the temperature of the room. In all, there are enormous amounts of environmental information that enters each child's sensory register. At this point, perception is important (Lerner, 2003), and is related to a child's past experiences and ability to organize and attach meaning to information.

In the information processing model, storage is the stage of memory used to describe information already received and perceived, and it can be short-term (sometimes referred to as working memory) or long term. Short-term memory has a storage capability that is temporary in nature. In order for information to go to long-term or permanent storage in long-term memory, the child must do something with the information such as link it to something already known or rehearse the information. For example, children may be better able to remember something they read when they focus on meaning, as opposed to trying to remember the words verbatim. This is why summarizing something in one's own words, or answering a question in one's own words, helps aid comprehension (Gunning, 2010). When information is learned and retained in long-term memory it is thought to be permanent. Long-term memory holds memory related to experiences (episodic) and information that is more verbal (semantic). The compilation of those memories, both experiences and knowledge, are the sum of our prior knowledge.

However, sometimes the difficulty occurs at the point of retrieval—bringing forth a stored memory. Retrieval is the process of accessing and transfering information stored in long-term memory to working memory so that it can be used. Deeper processing of information is thought to aid memory retrieval, and dual coding is a term that refers to processing a memory in more than one way (usually visually and verbally). Dual coding is thought to make retrieval more likely since the memory may be retrieved either verbally or visually. That is, there is more than one way to access the memory.

Memory has been found to be related to the development of early literacy skills and can be categorized in terms of auditory memory and visual memory. Phonological short-term memory refers to the ability to remember auditory information in the short term. This is another skill that the National Early Literacy Panel (2008) noted as predictive of later literacy skill development. The panel found that research results support the idea that efficient phonological short term memory skills are involved in literacy development. This skill has to do with the efficiency of storing information heard in the short term so that the information is available for use in working memory—so that something can be done with the information.

Similarly, the National Early Literacy Panel (NELP) (2008) reported that tasks such as rapid naming of letters and digits, and rapid naming of objects and colors were also consistently predictive of later conventional literacy results. Rapid naming tasks are also a function of memory and require an efficient retrieval system so that the information is available for use. This is a complex process that involves visual recognition, working memory, and oral language skills.

In addition, the ability to write letters of the alphabet in isolation upon request or the ability to write one's own name are tasks that research has shown to be predictive of later literacy outcomes (NELP, 2008). These tasks also require a combination of processes working in concert. First, the child must comprehend the request. Then the child must retrieve from memory the visual representation of the specific letter or sequence of letters in his/her name, and in the final step, the child must use fine motor skills to create that form on paper.

Memory plays an important, and perhaps underestimated, role in both early skill acquisition and later literacy proficiency. The following suggestions may be helpful in planning appropriate instruction for children and are illustrated in Figure 2.1. First, it is essential that teachers set a purpose (intention) for learning and help children activate strategies for retention. Children also need to have the opportunity for clear meaningful encoding. Therefore, it is best to avoid competition for attention and distractions when at all possible. Children may also benefit from instruction in mnemonics (memory tricks). In addition, teachers can organize and extend information to be learned, both visually and verbally, and provide examples.

Figure 2.1. Memory and Instruction.

Teachers should make sure that children have many opportunities for practice so skills are over-learned, or practiced beyond the acquisition phase of learning. Finally, it is often beneficial to provide rest or breaks after intensive learning sessions.

In sum, theories provide a way to view, examine, and make sense of the world. Specific to learning and literacy, theories help explain the processes of skill acquisition as children travel along the road to becoming expert readers and writers, and theories can provide a framework to understand the problems and find appropriate solutions to the struggles that some children face along the way. In this way theories can be very helpful in guiding literacy instruction.

LANGUAGE DEVELOPMENT

Language is a highly developed system of communication that serves as a means to communicate ideas, thoughts, and feelings with others. Language provides a community of people with a way to transmit culture from generation to generation. Therefore, language is a social phenomenon and includes both receptive and expressive components. The development of language is an amazing process and foundational to literacy. In fact, language competence appears to be strongly related to success in learning to read and write (Moats, 2010; Catts, & Kamhi, 2005). Several aspects of oral language in particular seem to be predictive of later conventional literacy skills, and these include grammar, definitional vocabulary, and listening comprehension (NELP, 2008). Furthermore, many refer to the concept of literacy in terms of language competencies. For example, Polloway and Smith (2003) suggest that literacy is the set of competencies children develop with both oral and printed language (including listening, speaking, reading, and writing) in order to succeed in school and in their lives outside of school.

In today's workforce, it is true that of the most desired skills employers want their employees to possess, language skills are directly involved in many of these skills. For instance, teamwork, interpersonal skills, oral communication, listening, leadership, writing, and reading are all language related skills that employers routinely seek in a potential employee. Not only is competence with language important to work life, but competence with language impacts how individuals form and maintain satisfying personal relationships. Real communication is possible when two things happen. First, the sender clearly expresses, either in writing or orally, such that the intended recipient is able to understand the precise meaning of the message. Second, the receiver accurately processes the language of the message, either through listening or reading. If there are difficulties with either the expressive or receptive sides of the language exchange, communication suffers and misunderstanding may result.

There are several language acquisition theories that address language development and can be conceptualized on the nature (genetics/biology) vs. nurture (environmental influences) continuum. At one end of the continuum, is the work of Noam Chomsky and the nativist view that language is genetic or innate to the person. According to Chomsky (1965) children are predisposed to acquire and use language. He posits that children have an inborn capacity for the linguistic universals common to all languages. This view suggests that children are born with the capacity to learn a set of transformational rules rather than just a string of words.

At the other end of the continuum is the work of B.F. Skinner and the behaviorist view that language is a result of what happens in the child's environment. That is, language is learned through imitation and reinforcement. For example, when an infant says his or her first word (e.g., *mama* or *dada*) parents positively reinforce the behavior with their excited reactions (cheers, inflected tone, smiles, etc.) and increase the probability that the behavior will be repeated in the future. The interactionist view (and the view of this book) falls somewhere between the two previous views of language acquisition and suggests that language development is the result of the interaction of biological abilities and environmental influences.

There are five important areas of language to understand. These five areas include phonology, morphology, syntax, semantics, and pragmatics. The first important area of language, phonology, is the system or set of rules governing how sounds are used to make syllables and words. Phonological awareness is an umbrella term used to describe a child's overall understanding of sounds in language. Phonology includes concepts such as phonemes, syllables, and onset and rime. A phoneme is the smallest distinguishable speech sound, and the English language has approximately 44 phonemes. For example, the word *man* is made up of the following three phonemes or distinct speech sounds /m/ /a/ /n/. When children are able to hear or distinguish the individual speech sounds in words, they have phonemic awareness. Phonemic awareness is important not only in oral language, but also in learning to read and spell.

The second important area of language is morphology. Morphology is the set of rules governing how syllables and words are formed to convey meaning. A morpheme is the smallest unit in language that carries meaning. Morphemes are used to indicate grammatical constructions such as tense, person, and number, and they are used to form adverbs and adjectives from root words. For example, the word *dog* has one morphological unit or morpheme, while the word *dogs* has two morphemes (*dog* + *s*), the plural form; and the word *call* has one morpheme, while the word *called* has two morphemes (*call* + *ed*), the past tense form.

Syntax is the study of linguistic conventions for the creation of meaningful sentences and phrases and is the set of rules governing word order. In English, the order of words is important in determining what the words actually mean. For example, syntax is involved in the grammatical construction of sentences in terms of the differences between statements, questions, and commands. The same words may be used in a statement and a question, but the order of the words helps convey the intended meaning. Thus, "Sam is reading the book" has a different meaning from "Is Sam reading the book?"

Semantics is the part of language that has to do with content or the meaning level of language and primarily involves vocabulary development. Semantics is the linguistic representation of things, events, ideas, processes, feelings, and relationships and is the area of language that allows a child to attribute meaning to his or her world and experiences. Semantic development, or vocabulary growth, is a life long learning process. The more one interacts with other people, and the more one reads, the more opportunities there are for vocabulary growth.

The final area of language is pragmatics and is related to how language is used in social contexts. Pragmatics includes the conventions that govern how language is used in social situations and is based on cultural norms. For example, pragmatics has to do with the rules that govern the code-of-conduct for conversations and includes things such as turn-taking, body positioning, personal space, and eye contact. There are several nonverbal language characteristics that are closely associated with pragmatics. These consist of paralinguistics, proxemics, kinesics, and chronemics. Paralinguistics includes the speech characteristics of pitch and range of the voice, vocal intensity, emphasis, and intonation patterns. Proxemics is the physical distance between individuals in a communication interaction. Kinesics is the body and facial movements or expressions that are used in communication. Finally, chronemics has to do with the timing involved in communication and includes appropriate pausing and turn-taking. All these nonverbal language characteristics are involved in pragmatics.

A review of the stages of language development in young children birth through approximately age eleven is important to understanding how language development relates to and impacts cognitive development and literacy skill development, and the following is based on the work of Polloway, Smith, and Miller (2004).

The language stages include: prelinguistic, emerging language, developing language, and language for learning. It is noteworthy that the ages for the stages are in terms of general ranges. The prelinguistic stage is the first stage of language development and covers infancy from birth through approximately 12 months. During this stage of development the infant's means of expression is through facial expressions (such as smiling), babbling, vocal intonations (such as cooing), and visual gaze. Communication at the beginning of this stage is preintentional and transitions to intentional by the end.

The second stage is the emerging language stage and covers ages 12 months to 26 months. Children are beginning to use one and two-word phrases with an expressive vocabulary of approximately 50 words or more. The sounds or phonology is increasingly consistent. Children are naming important people, objects, and processes, and they have a variety of intentions or purposes for communicating. For example, typical words (in addition to *mama* and *dada*) that may be a part of a child's expressive language during this stage include: *no, all gone, stop, go, more, this, kiss, up, out, big, dog,* and *hi*. Two-word phrases typically indicate a simple association or cognitive process (i.e., *cat eat; Daddy truck; go bye bye).*

The next stage is the developing language stage and children from 27 to 46 months of age typically have an explosive growth in vocabulary. They are combining words into sentences of up to about five words and they are beginning to put together or retell stories. In addition, they are learning the social conventions of language.

In the language for learning stage (approximately 5 to 10 years of age), children typically continue to experience a tremendous growth in vocabulary that is more in-depth and broader in scope. They are transitioning from personal to shared meanings and are developing competence in conversation. In addition, children at this stage of language development are developing metalinguistic awareness—an ability to think about, talk about, and reflect on language.

In sum, the importance of language development to later literacy skill development cannot be overstated. Furthermore, problems in language development are evident in many children with learning disabilities (Lerner, 2003). It is essential that teachers model and then support critical language skills. One language skill that appears simple, yet is actually very challenging for children (and adults, too) is the skill of listening. The words, "Listen to my instructions more carefully", "You didn't listen", or "How many times have I told you?" are heard too often in many classrooms. Listening skills are vitally important. So much of instruction, especially in the early school years, is provided through language and requires good listening skills. Children need to be supported in developing their listening skills, and this includes helping children develop self-awareness and self-regulation so they understand that listening is an active process of thinking and interacting with the speaker. First, this process can be modeled by the teacher with a think-aloud, and then children should be given many opportunities to practice and develop their listening skills.

Language Activities for Early Childhood

- Play: Encourage dramatic play and narrate children's play using a story grammar; encourage play that incorporates the give and take of language (children taking on different roles and communicating in play); talk about talking; and play with language through songs and rhymes; play games that require active listening (e.g., *Simon Says*).
- Snack time: Encourage children to talk about food—their favorites, family dishes, and stories about food; and help children play with the sounds and words and meanings that are related to their snacks.
- Sharing time: Model how to share a personal story; incorporate *star* days so that each child has a chance to be the designated star of the day; encourage children to extend their oral expression by asking open ended questions; expand the child's language by recasting (not overtly correcting) their sentences into acceptable grammatical form.
- Read Alouds: Read stories with enthusiasm; point out the parts of a story's grammar (e.g., setting, characters, plot, etc.); do a picture walk and ask children to make predictions about the story; after a read-aloud encourage children to retell the story; read rhyming books and help children create their own rhymes to selected target words; share a wordless picture book with children and have them generate a story to go along with the pictures.

Language Activities for the Primary Grades

- All of the early childhood language activities may be expanded to support language development in the primary grades as well (e.g., read aloud to children and ask open-ended questions, encourage oral language expression through sharing and cooperative group work, and play with language through song and rhyme, etc.).
- Read-alouds: Have children listen to a story and then orally summarize the main idea/events sequentially to expand oral

expression (e.g., appropriate grammar and use of new vocabulary); have children talk about the language of the story; encourage children to relate the story events to something they already know about or have experienced (through small group discussions and writing).

- Language play: Play games with synonyms, homonyms, and antonyms; encourage students to create songs and poetry to present to younger classes; create classroom word walls; have secret message hunts; have children participate in creating "words of the day".

QUESTIONS FOR REFLECTION AND DISCUSSION

1) Think about a teacher who made a positive difference in your life. What qualities did that person possess? What did he or she do that made a difference? How did he or she make you feel?
2) What do the terms intrinsic motivation and extrinsic motivation mean? What is a specific example of intrinsic motivation from your own life? What is a specific example of extrinsic motivation from your own life?
3) Why do you want to be a teacher? Be specific.
4) What qualities do you already have and what qualities do you need to work on in order for you to be a great teacher?
5) Reflect on the following question. Am I a good listener? Give examples from your own life of times when you were a good listener and times when you were not a good listener.
6) How does a child know when an adult is really listening?
7) What roles do parents and families play in the language development of their young children?
8) How can teachers help children improve their language skills?

CHAPTER APPLICATION EXERCISES

1) Brainstorm ways to create a safe, supportive, and joyful learning environment. Create a graphic organizer to represent your ideas.
2) Interview a school administrator about the qualities they look for in hiring new teachers. Write a one-page summary of your findings.

3) In your collaborative group, design a game to reinforce correct use of syntax in sentences for use in a primary (grade one or two) classroom. Create a title for your game and then list the materials needed to construct the game, write directions for constructing the game, and include instructions for playing the game.

4) Develop a language evaluation checklist for a kindergarten classroom based on information obtained from a reputable website. Be prepared to share your findings with others.

Chapter 3

SPECIAL EDUCATION AND GENERAL EDUCATION

"Example is not the main thing in influencing others. It is the only thing."
(Albert Schweitzer)

INCLUSIVE CLASSROOMS

Today, there is an assumption that children with disabilities will be educated in neighborhood schools, in general education settings, with their non-disabled peers to the greatest extent possible. This idea has become known as inclusion. The basic assumption or philosophy of inclusion is found in language in the Individuals with Disabilities Education Act (IDEA, 2004) and directly relates to the concept of least-restrictive environment (LRE). The inclusion movement was advanced by civil rights and social justice ideals. That is, special education reformers of the 1980's and 1990's argued that children with disabilities should not be denied access to general education classrooms and hence an appropriate education (Ferguson, 2008). Although there is variation in rates among the states, according to the recent U.S. Department of Education Institute of Educational Sciences report (2010), *Condition of Education, Children and Youth with Disabilities*, about 95 percent of children and youth aged 6-21 who were served under IDEA in 2007-08 were enrolled in regular schools, and the national average for school age children with disabilities who spent at least 80% of their day in general education grew from 32% in the 1989-90 school year, to 57% by the 2007-08 school year.

Historically, a variety of service options (physical locations) that vary along a continuum has been the focus of LRE—everything from fulltime in the general education classroom to residential schools. However, LRE also must consider the instructional and social contexts of placements (Bateman, 2007; Zigmond, Kloo, & Volonino, 2009), meaning that meeting each child's needs should be the primary concern, rather than promoting full-inclusion as the best option for all students. According to Kauffman et al. (2008),

> The most effective service delivery system probably cannot be defined totally in the abstract, for it likely depends on the characteristics of the student (e.g., age, type and severity of disability), the qualifications of the teacher(s) who will provide instruction, other students with whom a student will be grouped, and features of the placement. Our view is that there is probably not a single, best delivery system, but a variety of arrangements suited to make maximum use of the student's abilities. Those who propose a single best solution in all cases (e.g., self-contained special class, inclusion in general education with collaboration and consultation of all concerned parties) are in our opinion misguided. (p. 372)

Furthermore, just because a child is included in a general education classroom does not mean that he or she has real membership in the learning or social community of the classroom. Truly inclusive education means that teachers must take responsibility for the educational needs of all children in their classrooms (intellectual, social, and emotional). This is not an easy task, and the best course of action has been the target of much heart-felt debate. Critical to the concept of inclusion has been a reexamination of the roles and responsibilities of teachers, both general and special education. The result has been the proliferation of the co-teaching service delivery model where the special education teacher and general education teacher work together within an individual classroom (Scruggs, Mastropieri, McDuffie, 2007; Volonio & Zigmond, 2007). Although there are several configurations possible within co-teaching models, in a recent metasynthesis of co-teaching classrooms the most common teaching role configuration was the "one teach, one assist" with the special educator taking the role of the assistant (see Scruggs, Mastropieri, & McDuffie, 2007). This raises concerns about the quality of special education services within general education classrooms. According to Volonio and Zigmond (2007),

> Observations of co-taught classrooms indicate that the general education teacher typically retains responsibility for teaching academic content, and the special educator, at best, provides scaffolding and support...There is little evidence that such assisting practices improve student learning, particularly among students considered exceptional or at-risk. (p. 298)

Similarly, Scruggs, Mastropieri, and McDuffie (2007, p. 412) examined co-teaching in inclusive classrooms and found that, "Practices known to be effective and frequently recommended—such as peer mediation, strategy instruction, mnemonics, study skills training, self-advocacy skills training, self-monitoring, ...were only rarely observed." In addition, while there is research evidence that direct, and systematic instruction in reading is beneficial for students with learning and behavioral disabilities (Vaughn & Linan-Thompson, 2003; Carnine, Silbert, Kame'enui, & Tarver, 2010), direct instruction is more the exception than the norm in general education settings (Zigmond, Kloo, & Volonino, 2009; Swanson, 2008).

Therefore, the question of whether or not students with disabilities are receiving an appropriate education remains a critical one. According to IDEA (2004), an appropriate education includes specially designed instruction that is designed to meet the unique needs of a child with a disability. In fact, the case may be made that children with disabilities are unlikely to reach their full potential without a special education program that is designed to address their specific needs and abilities (Lunenberg, 2010). To this end, special education really is special—with special instructional procedures, materials, equipment, or facilities (Kaufman & Wandberg, 2010). According to Kauffman and Hallahan (2005), even the best of general education classrooms cannot replace special education programs, because special education is more precise and more controlled in instructional contexts with regard to such things as pace of instruction, rate of response, intensity, relentlessness, structure, reinforcement, teacher-pupil ratio, monitoring procedures, and assessments.

CHARACTERISTICS OF LEARNERS WITH SPECIAL NEEDS

Each child comes to school with his or her own unique personality, temperament, cognitive abilities, and life experiences. In this section, some characteristics that are commonly observed in children with special needs will be addressed. By definition, children who qualify for special education services, regardless of their disability category, are in need of specialized instruction, materials, or services in order to reach their full potential. Thus, a primary concern for students with special needs is that they have learning differences or difficulties that must be considered in planning and designing instruction. Therefore, each child in special education has an individualized education plan (IEP) based on his or her specific characteristics and needs.

Teachers should be aware of some relevant cognitive, affective, and behavioral characteristics and considerations. For example, many children with special needs often demonstrate deficits in the following cognitive tasks: memory; metacognition (the ability to think about one's own thinking); and motivation. According to Hallahan, Kauffman, and Pullen (2010), one of the reasons children with disabilities have difficulty with memory tasks is because they fail to use strategies, such as rehearsal or chunking, to help them remember. In reading, the failure to use metacognitive skills may be evident when children fail to monitor their comprehension of a passage. They may not have or use any strategies to discover whether or not they understand a given passage. Motivation to read may also be a stumbling block for children with disabilities. Teachers should take into consideration that when children have opportunities to experience success, with a variety of personally interesting materials, they are more likely to be motivated to read.

Similarly, many children with special needs often display difficulties in affective skill areas such as social skills, and self-concept. Additionally, children with special needs may exhibit deficits in the behavioral realm such as: disruptive behavior, withdrawal, and adaptive behavior or life skills.

High incidence disabilities are those disabilities that occur most frequently in the population. Within high incidence disabilities is the special education category known as learning disabilities (LD). What are learning disabilities and how are they defined? Over the years there has been a lack of consensus in a single acceptable definition—not all groups have the same definition. For example, the Individuals with Disabilities Education Act (IDEA), defines learning disability as follows:

> (i) General. The term means a disorder in one or more of the basic psychological processes involved in understanding or in using language, spoken or written, that may manifest itself in an imperfect ability to listen, think, speak, read, write, spell, or to do mathematical calculations, including conditions such as perceptual disabilities, brain injury, minimal brain dysfunction, dyslexia, and developmental aphasia.
>
> (ii) Disorders not included. The term does not include learning problems that are primarily the result of visual, hearing, or motor disabilities, of mental retardation, of emotional disturbance, or of environmental, cultural, or economic disadvantage (Section 300.7(c)(10) of 34 CFR Parts 300 and 303)

The definition provided above is based on the U.S. federal laws and regulations, while the following definition from the National Joint Committee on Learning Disabilities (NJCLD, 1990) states:

> Learning disabilities is a general term that refers to a heterogeneous group of disorders manifested by significant difficulties in the acquisition and use of listening, speaking, reading, writing, reasoning, or mathematical abilities. These disorders are intrinsic to the individual, presumed to be due to central nervous system dysfunction, and may occur across the life span. Problems in self-regulatory behaviors, social perception, and social interaction may exist with learning disabilities but do not by themselves constitute a learning disability. Although learning disabilities may occur concomitantly with other handicapping conditions (for example, sensory impairment, mental retardation, serious emotional disturbance), or with extrinsic influences (such as cultural differences, insufficient or inappropriate instruction), they are not the result of those conditions or influences.

In other words, children with LD have difficulty acquiring basic skills or academic content. It is important to understand that the overarching concept of LD includes more than a single condition, and includes many different characteristics. Each child with LD has his or her own unique set of characteristic learning or behavioral traits. Although there are some common traits, no one child will exhibit all of the traits. Moreover, certain characteristics are more likely to be displayed at certain age levels, and these characteristics may manifest in different ways at various age levels.

Many children with LD have underlying language difficulties that can have an impact on oral language, reading, and writing (See Polloway, & Smith, 2004). Children who have oral language difficulties display problems in speaking or listening, or both. One of the most common and significant characteristics exhibited by many students with LD is difficulty with reading development. It has been estimated that approximately 80 percent of children with LD have problems with reading (Learner, 2003), specifically in the skill areas of decoding, fluency, and reading comprehension (Hallahan, et al., 2005). Additionally, many children with LD experience significant problems with written expression. Although some children with LD have their primary difficulties in math, these problems are beyond the scope of this book.

Children with LD often have intra-individual differences that may be observed across academic areas. For example, a child may demonstrate competence in math computation and listening comprehension, yet may exhibit difficulty with word identification and reading comprehension. Other students may read and speak well but have difficulty expressing their thoughts in writing (See http://www.teachingld.org).

Dyslexia is another term that is often used (and often misunderstood) to discuss the characteristics of a subgroup of children who have LD—those who have specific difficulties with reading. Spafford and Grosser (2005) provide the following definition of dyslexia:

> "Dyslexia" definition = *dys* and *lexia*, or the inability to effectively read words, is the most prevalent specific learning disability (at least 50% of the LD population). It is thought to have a neurological basis, and the disability is unexpected in relation to other cognitive abilities and access to effective classroom instruction. There are specific difficulties with fluent reading and the phonological components of language (i.e., phonemic awareness). Secondary issues may or may not include other academic problems (e.g., reading comprehension); difficulties in socialization (e.g., more negative peer interactions) and co-existing disabilities or disorders (e.g., ADD or ADHD with 25% of those with dyslexia). With intensive literacy support in reading and

writing, a social-academic network of support, and the development of individual resiliency, individuals with dyslexia can lead successful and fulfilling lives. (p. 2)

There are several additional issues that teachers should consider when designing and planning literacy instruction, in particular for students with special needs. These include engagement, attribution, and self-efficacy for school related activities. Engagement refers to how involved a child is in the learning process. Sometimes children with special needs are characterized as being passive or inactive learners (Rivera & Smith, 1997). An inactive learner is not actively engaged, is not well-organized, and lacks appropriate strategies to approach school tasks. Students with LD often have difficulty working independently, have difficulty with homework, and do not know or use strategies to tackle academic problems (Hallahan et al., 2005). The good news is these skills can be taught.

Attribution refers to the reason a child attributes as a cause of his or her success or failure. Children with LD may have an external locus of control so that they believe things happen because of external factors such as luck instead of internal factors such as determination and hard work. For example, after taking a weekly quiz one child attributes his lack of success to bad luck, while another child attributes her success to having spent time studying for the quiz. The internal factor can be controlled (the amount of time spent studying), while the other external factor (bad luck) cannot. Children who believe that their lives are controlled by external factors may develop learned helplessness, a term used to describe the tendency to give up and not try any longer. Children can be helped to improve skills through specific skill instruction, strategy use, and concerted effort and time spent on a task. Then they begin to attribute their successes to hard work.

Self-efficacy is a related concept and has to do with how children feel about themselves in a particular area such as reading. Self-efficacy often varies among school subjects. For example, a child may have low reading self-efficacy due to a history of unsuccessful experiences, yet the same child may have high music self-efficacy, and high math self-efficacy. Due to a history of difficulties in reading, confidence levels may be low for students with special needs, and as a result they do not enjoy reading. Thus, their reader self-efficacy is impacted in a negative way. Self-efficacy for reading refers to how well a child thinks he or she can accomplish a particular reading task. Reader self-efficacy is influenced by how well children have performed on similar tasks in the past, including any accompanying feedback and encouragement received (Wigfield, Guthrie, Tonks, & Perencevich, 2004), and reader self-efficacy is an important aspect of making the transition from novice to expert reader. Children's self-perceptions (i.e., reader self-efficacy) are important to consider and are influential components of who they are as learners. In other words, children are sensitive in their views of themselves as readers and their views are important to the learning process. Furthermore, setting goals and attaining goals is important, and because children who struggle with reading do not automatically self-evaluate their abilities accurately, teachers can prompt them to assess performance and gauge their progress toward goals to increase reader self-efficacy and motivation (Ferrara, 2005). If teachers know readers' self-efficacy levels, know what they attribute their successes and failures to, and know how engaged they are as learners, they can plan instruction accordingly to meet those needs.

RESPONSE TO INTERVENTION

Response to intervention (RTI) is a policy initiative that has gained the support of many—although there are variations in the interpretation and implementation of RTI. For the purposes of this book, RTI will be discussed in terms of how it can be used to promote early intervention practices, as well as aid in valid disability identification.

RTI is a general education initiative that is designed as a preventative measure against academic difficulty and ultimately academic failure. RTI is a tiered educational process that incorporates evidence-based instruction, monitoring of all student progress, and additional support for students who need it. RTI is used to determine whether or not children are responding to instruction and making progress. RTI matches instructional support (instructional interventions) to a child's individual needs through a multi-tier model that increases in intensity in each subsequent tier.

Although RTI and the specific manner of implementation are left to the states, there are a number of commonalities. First, appropriate instruction (scientific, research-based instruction) should be delivered to children in the general education classroom by qualified personnel. Second, universal screening should be used to identify children who are not making academic progress at the expected rate (grade-level). In addition, instruction should be matched to individual children's needs and should include targeted interventions that increase in intensity with each successive level or tier. RTI includes progress monitoring by the use of repeated assessment—including curriculum based measures (CBM). Finally, parents will be informed of the interventions and the results.

The specific underlying critical features of the RTI model include the following:

1) universal screening;
2) measurable target behavior or problem;
3) collection of baseline data prior to introduction of an intervention;
4) a written plan;
5) progress monitoring;
6) comparison of pre and post-intervention data (analysis of results).

One of the central features of RTI is that the initial focus is on improving core classroom instruction through the integration of assessment and high quality teaching based on scientific research results. Tier 1 is the first layer in the RTI process, and the emphasis is on providing all children with appropriate instruction (by the classroom teacher) in the general education classroom. Instruction is evidence-based meaning that the instructional methods and materials are based on educational research showing that these methods are effective. This is considered to be scientific research-based core instruction. Core instruction is the term used to denote that this is the primary intervention and is used for all students in the general education setting.

RTI begins with the universal screening of all students at the beginning of the school year. Screening assessments quickly measure all students in the skills expected for grade level and are usually conducted three times a year. Screening assessments are used to identify students who are potentially at risk for school failure.

According to Fuchs, Fuchs, and Stecker (2010,), when the results of the screening indicate that a child may be at risk,

> ...academic performance is then monitored weekly from 5 to 8 weeks as the teacher implements evidence-based (generally effective) instruction. This constitutes Tier 1 of the RTI model. Nonresponsive children move to Tier 2, which offers tutoring in small groups by an adult using a standard treatment protocol. This often scripted, or partly scripted protocol—of which many exist for early reading...has typically been tested in one or more randomized controlled study or quasi-experimental study. (p. 302)

The Tier 2 intervention includes the specific teaching method/strategy, an increase in the intensity of the intervention, and the duration of the intervention (how long the intervention will be provided). Increased intensity can include the following: An increase in how often instruction is provided (additional time spent in instruction); a decrease in the instructional group size (smaller groups, pairs, or even one-on-one instruction); and/or more instruction focused on specific skill areas.

A team approach is generally used to determine the level of support needed for each student. In general, the team is made of the child's classroom teacher, other teachers as appropriate (such as the reading teacher), and staff (such as the school psychologist), and parent(s). The RTI team recommends the type of instructional support (standard protocol) and how often progress will be monitored. Progress monitoring is an important step in the RTI process because it helps the team see if the instructional support is working or if it needs to be changed. Progress may be monitored once a week, bi-weekly, or more often depending on the level of the intervention and student need. The progress results are plotted on a graph and tracked over time for a visual evaluation of results. The progress monitoring results of Tier 2 and Tier 3 targeted interventions should be made available to parents so they can see and understand the instructional support and progress of their child.

Tier 2, the second level of intervention in RTI is intended for the estimated 10-15% of children who do not make adequate progress with the core instruction in the first tier. Instruction at this level is given by specially trained personnel and designed to promote the acquisition of new skills. A Tier 2 intervention is supplemental—an add-on. That is, instruction is provided in addition to what the child receives as part of his or her general education class. This may be done within the classroom or in another location.

Fuchs, Fuchs, and Stecker, (2010) state,

> The specialized training [of personnel], together with the explicitness of the instruction and its empirical validation; the small and homogeneous student groups; and the greater frequency and duration of the tutoring sessions (minimally 8-10 weeks, 4 days per week, 30 min. per session) make Tier 2 more intensive than Tier 1. (p. 303)

The RTI model also includes on-going support to the classroom teacher. Typically, a child in Tier 2 will receive the following: Instruction in a small group setting; evidence-based instruction; additional opportunities for practice; and more intensive instruction in problem areas. In order to determine if the intervention is working to improve the child's skills, progress is regularly assessed and monitored. Furthermore, Tier 2 level instruction tests a student's responsiveness to instructional practices that are usually effective (Fuchs, Fuchs, & Stecker, 2010).

If the student responds to the instruction in Tier 2, he or she returns to Tier 1, in other words, general class instruction. However, when progress monitoring indicates that the child is not making adequate progress in Tier 2, the next level in

RTI is Tier 3. This third level of instructional intervention is intended for children (about 1-5%) who are not responding to the interventions of Tier 1 and Tier 2. When a child does not make the expected progress in Tier 2, further evaluation may be required to determine if the student needs special education services. That is, students who do not respond to Tier 2 instruction are evaluated by multidisciplinary teams to identify students' strengths and needs and to explore eligibility for Tier 3 (special education services). The information gathered throughout the RTI process is used as additional information in this comprehensive evaluation. In this model of RTI, instruction in Tier 3 (special education) is even more intensive. The intensiveness may include more frequent instruction, for a longer duration, smaller instructional groups, and different materials or programs which focus specifically on areas of individual need. For example a child may receive instruction in a Tier 3 targeted intervention in a small (homogeneous) group or individually, for a minimum of 30 minutes per day outside of the classroom, for 6-12 weeks. Progress in Tier 3 is monitored frequently.

RTI is an important systematic and data-driven educational model that is designed to address the learning needs of all students. Adjustments to instructional interventions are made according to the data, so that children who have difficulty with one instructional method are given the opportunity to be successful with another. RTI is a prevention model in that it seeks to prevent smaller achievement gaps from becoming insurmountable gaps by finding learning difficulties early and addressing them immediately. That is, the RTI model identifies children who are struggling before they fall behind or fail. Additionally, because RTI is a scientifically research-based model, there are major potential benefits in the identification and use of appropriate interventions for students with learning disabilities.

STRENGTHENING THE RTI FRAMEWORK

What follows is based on the work of Fuchs, Fuchs, and Stecker (2010), in which they suggest that the most intensive tier of the RTI framework should be special education and should include experimental teaching in an effort to best address the needs of nonresponders. In this conceptualization, experimental teaching is used to collect ongoing data that are graphed for ease of interpretation, and then instructional decisions are made based on these data. Any instructional changes are noted on the student's graph and entered into a separate phase on the chart. The student's Individualized Education Program (IEP) goals are used to draw trend lines so that it is easy to visually determine whether or not progress is being made toward the IEP goals during each of the phases.

In practice this conceptualization of RTI and experimental teaching is very similar to single-subject research design. One particular single subject research design that may be of benefit to educators as they seek to find ways to help nonresponders is known as the changing criterion design (See Tawny & Gast, 1989).

Special education is truly special and it is imperative that special educators renew their commitment to the mission of helping those children who struggle the most to develop the skills that will allow them to reach their potential as independent, productive, and fulfilled human beings. Fuchs, Fuchs, and Stecker (2010, p. 318) suggest that special educators should once again determine that "their historic mission is to work with the most difficult to teach children and youth and that their professional roots are in the instructional methods of clinical teaching."

CURRICULUM BASED MEASUREMENT

Two related terms are essential to the discussion of special education and general education, and these are curriculum based measurement (CBM) and continuous progress monitoring (CPM). Continuous progress monitoring is one of the critical features of RTI previously discussed. However, CPM is broader in that academic skills of all students are assessed on a regular basis so that skill acquisition can be monitored and documented, and the information can help focus instruction and differentiate instructional groupings. The other related term, curriculum based measurement (CBM), is a way to monitor (measure and document) children's progress in areas such as reading, mathematics, and written expression. CBM is often used because the measures are quick, as well as inexpensive to administer, are sensitive to small changes over brief time intervals, are reliable and valid indicators of achievement, and can be used to guide instructional decisions. The Dynamic Indicators of Early Literacy Skills (DIBELS) is one such instrument with subtests measures such as: Initial sound fluency; letter naming fluency; phoneme segmentation fluency; nonsense word fluency; oral reading fluency, etc. (See http://www.uoregon.edu/ for more information).

In a reading CBM, children are given short graded passages of connected text (approximately 250 words). Typically the child is asked to read three passages that are of equal difficulty at approximately his/her instructional reading level

(95% accuracy or greater). The child's reading rate is timed and accuracy levels recorded, resulting in a score for words read correctly per minute, and a score for error words per minute. Another CBM that is often utilized in reading is the maze procedure. The maze is used to assess reading comprehension. Again, the child is given a graded passage at his or her instructional reading level. The child is given a specific time period to read the passage (usually 3 minutes). The text contains blanks (approximately every 7 or so words), with multiple choice options. The student circles the word that best makes sense in each opportunity to respond. The score is the number of correct words circled in the allotted time period. This CBM is a measure of comprehension.

THE FIVE ESSENTIAL ELEMENTS OF LITERACY INSTRUCTION

Comprehensive literacy programs include instruction in phonemic awareness, phonics, vocabulary, fluency, and comprehension. In addition, they incorporate state learning standards, make use of evidence-based practices, use assessments to monitor progress and plan future instruction, and consistently link reading and writing activities. Each of the essential elements is presented in the following chapters.

QUESTIONS FOR REFLECTION AND DISCUSSION

1) Explain and discuss the Response to Intervention (RTI) framework as it applies to literacy. What happens within each tier?
2) How can teachers meet the needs of children with special needs in inclusive classrooms?
3) What is CBM and how can it be used to support the learning of struggling readers?

CHAPTER APPLICATION EXERCISES

1) Read two research articles about inclusion of students with disabilities and the teaching of literacy skills. Write a short one-page paper summarizing your findings.

2) Observe a primary inclusive classroom during their literacy block. Pay particular attention to how the classroom is set up, the schedule, and how lessons are conducted with all children. Be ready to share your observations.

Chapter 4

PHONOLOGICAL AWARENESS AND PHONICS

"Hop, Pop. We like to hop. We like to hop on top of Pop."
Theodor Geisel (Dr. Seuss)

PHONOLOGICAL AWARENESS

Phonological awareness is a term used to refer to the abilities needed to recognize, manipulate, or analyze the parts of spoken language (e.g., sentences, words, syllables, and phonemes). These have been found to be foundational skills implicated in later literacy development (National Reading Panel, 2000). Although the terms phonological awareness and phonemic awareness are sometimes used interchangeably, there is a distinct difference. Thus, for the sake of clarity these terms will be used here to illustrate defined circumstances.

Phonological awareness is the broader term—more of an umbrella term. Phonological awareness, as the term implies, has to do with the sounds of spoken language. Children become aware that what is spoken can be written down and that words are distinct units of language. Furthermore, children learn that sentences are made up of words, words have parts or syllables, and they begin to hear and distinguish characteristics of language (e.g., rhyming and alliteration). The development of these language skills is important to later literacy development.

Phonemic awareness is the more specific term and relates to the ability to hear the individual speech sounds within words. Similar to phonological awareness, the skill is an auditory skill. However phonemic awareness focuses down to the level of the individual and specific sounds within a spoken word. Children learn to hear the individual speech sounds within a given word, and they develop the ability to recognize, isolate, and manipulate those sounds. Some children seem to gain these skills with little or no effort, while many other children need support, direct instruction, and many opportunities for practicing the newly learned skills. To encourage and support phonological awareness abilities (including phonemic awareness), activities should involve playing and having fun with language.

Current research on the important underlying skills needed in learning to read and write consistently point to well-developed phonological awareness skills and alphabet knowledge, as well as point to the need for explicit and systematic instruction in these underlying skills (Carnine, Silbert, Kame'enui, & Tarver, 2010; National Early Literacy Panel, 2008). The terms explicit and systematic are crucial in the "how" of the instructional process—to make sure children have the best opportunities to successfully build the foundational skills necessary for reading and writing. Explicit instruction is instruction that is not based on assumptions. That is, explicit instruction incorporates demonstrations and modeling, and provides explanation and support when needed. When this approach is taken, skill development is not left to chance. Systematic instruction means that the instruction is well-planned, logical in sequence, has measurable objectives, and provides children with abundant opportunities for practice.

With regard to phonological awareness skills and early childhood education (birth to age 5), the National Early Literacy Panel (2008) suggests that there are key skills that can serve as reliable and stable indicators for monitoring a child's progress toward developing conventional literacy skills. In addition, the National Early Literacy Panel findings indicate that instruction that focuses on phonological awareness in general, and phonemic awareness in particular, may provide valuable literacy preparation for children who may be at risk of failing to attain basic literacy skill development. The findings have implications for school-age children and preschoolers. Elementary educators and early childhood educators have a responsibility to insure the best possible literacy outcomes for all children. Thus, teachers must have an understanding of phonemic awareness and how phonemic awareness relates to the teaching of reading and writing.

WHAT IS A PHONEME?

By definition, a phoneme is a perceptually distinctive unit of sound in a language (Mish, 1994). Similarly, the National Reading Panel (2000) defines phonemes as the smallest units composing spoken language. For example, the beginning sound /k/ in cat and the beginning sound /k/ in kite have the same single distinctive sound. Phonemic awareness is the ability to recognize, isolate, and manipulate the single distinctive sounds in words and syllables. The process of becoming phonemically aware helps children understand that words are made up of sequences of speech sounds. Phonemic awareness is the first step in the process and helps children understand that spoken language can be written down with symbols (graphemes) known as letters. Children begin to make sense of the alphabet. That is, children begin to understand that the letters in words are systematically related to the sounds of language. This is often referred to as the sound-symbol code. Understanding the sound-symbol code, the alphabetic principle, gives children a way to approach sounding out and reading new words, as well as a foundation for how to write (spell) what they want to convey as beginning writers. Alphabetic awareness is explored in detail later in the chapter.

The process of becoming aware of the sounds in words appears to be a simple enough process. However, phonemic awareness is sometimes less than intuitive. For example, there are approximately 40-44 phonemes or single distinctive sounds in the English language. In contrast there are only 26 letters in the alphabet. It is important to note that the number of phonemes varies across sources. To complicate matters, these distinctive sounds are represented with approximately 250 different spellings. In addition, many phonemes are not obvious and must be taught because the sounds in words are oftentimes co-articulated. This means the sounds are not obviously distinctly separate from one another (Carnine, et al., 2010). Is it any wonder, some children have difficulty learning to read and write? The University of Oregon's Institute for Development of Educational Achievement website, www.uoregon.edu, (2009) suggests the following phonological awareness benchmarks for kindergarten: 25 first sounds per minute by mid-year, and 35 sound segments per minute by the end of kindergarten. Additionally they suggest that by the end of kindergarten, children should be able to do the following: discriminate sounds or words as alike or different; distinguish and produce rhyming words; orally blend syllables, parts of words (onsets and rimes) and phonemes into whole words; count or physically clap or tap out the words in a 3-5 word sentence and the syllables in up to 3-syllable words. They also suggest that by the end of kindergarten, children should be able to pronounce the individual syllables in 2 and 3 syllable words; identify the beginning sound in one syllable words; and segment 2 and 3 phoneme words into their individual sounds.

According to the National Early Literacy Panel (2008), it is important that children become progressively more able to deal with smaller and smaller units of sound. This means that as children begin to become aware of the sounds of language they should progress from the larger units of sound such as sentences and words to smaller units such as syllables and onset/rimes all the way down to the smallest unit, the phoneme. The report also suggests that phonological awareness training is likely to help children develop the early skills related to later literacy achievement, and although phonological awareness activities may be conducted alone, combining these with other activities that build print knowledge is likely to be additionally beneficial.

PHONOLOGICAL AWARENESS: INSTRUCTIONAL PRACTICES

One of the best ways to encourage the growth of phonological awareness is to focus on and play with language sounds through children's poetry, songs, rhymes, and chants (Rasinski, Pakak, & Fawcett, 2010). In addition, more specific phonemic awareness activities can be sequenced, from simple to more advanced, to help prepare children to understand the alphabetic principle or letter-sound correspondences. Such activities include phoneme matching, phoneme isolation, phoneme blending, phoneme segmentation, and phoneme manipulation (See Figure 4.1).

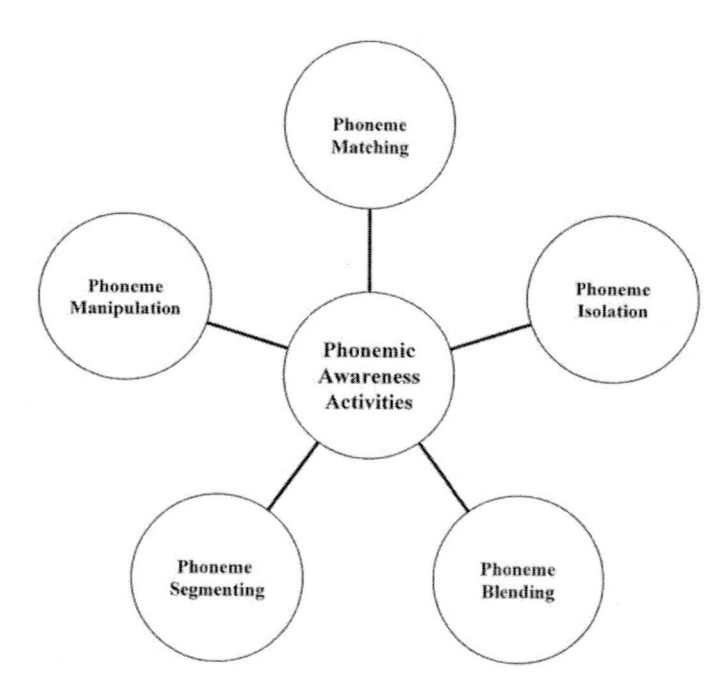

Figure 4.1. Phonemic Awareness Activities.

PHONEMIC AWARENESS ACTIVITIES

- Phoneme matching: Children determine whether or not initial, medial, or final sounds in selected words are alike.

  o   The teacher might say, "Do bat and bear begin with the same sound?" or "Do pup and cup end with the same sound?"
  o   Game-like activities that require children match beginning sounds with picture cards are helpful and fun (see the Florida Center for Reading Research website www.fcrr.org /curriculum/pdf/GK-1/F for a detailed activity example)

- Phoneme Isolation: Children isolate specific sounds in words.

  o   The teacher might say, "What is the first sound you hear in little?" or "What is the last sound you hear in man?"
  o   One website that may be of interest is the following: http: //www.readingrockets. org/article/

- Phoneme blending: Children blend sounds to form words.

  o   The teacher might say, "What word do the sounds /m/ /a/ /t/ make?" or "What word do the sounds /d/ /o/ /g/ make?"

- Phoneme segmentation: Children separate words into sounds.

  o   The teacher might say, "What sounds make up the word *cat*?" or "What sounds make up the word *lip*?"

- Phoneme manipulation: Children manipulate the sounds in words.

  o   The teacher might say, "Say the word *sit* without the /s/ sound" or "Say *pot* without the /t/ sound."
  o   One website that may be of interest is the following: http://www.readingresource.net/phonemicawarenessactivities.html

Reading aloud to children helps foster many language and literacy skills and is an enjoyable way to focus on the sounds of language. The following list of books in Figure 4.2 represents a starting point. There are many other books that play with language that are equally relevant and deserve attention.

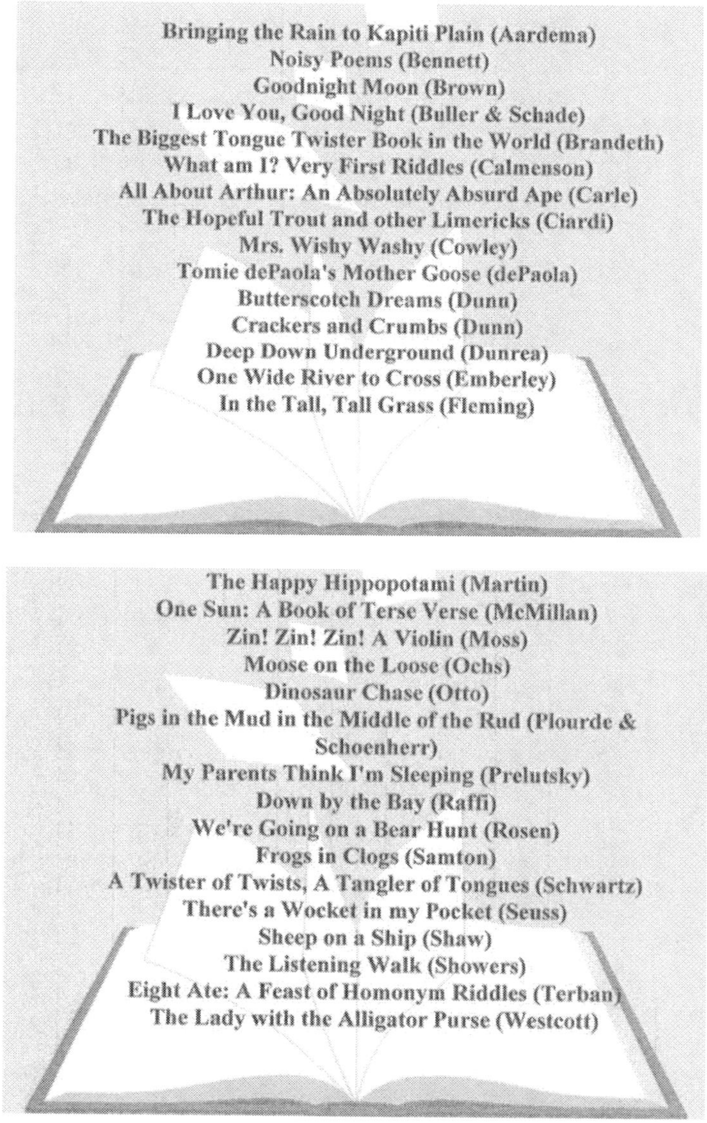

Bringing the Rain to Kapiti Plain (Aardema)
Noisy Poems (Bennett)
Goodnight Moon (Brown)
I Love You, Good Night (Buller & Schade)
The Biggest Tongue Twister Book in the World (Brandeth)
What am I? Very First Riddles (Calmenson)
All About Arthur: An Absolutely Absurd Ape (Carle)
The Hopeful Trout and other Limericks (Ciardi)
Mrs. Wishy Washy (Cowley)
Tomie dePaola's Mother Goose (dePaola)
Butterscotch Dreams (Dunn)
Crackers and Crumbs (Dunn)
Deep Down Underground (Dunrea)
One Wide River to Cross (Emberley)
In the Tall, Tall Grass (Fleming)

The Happy Hippopotami (Martin)
One Sun: A Book of Terse Verse (McMillan)
Zin! Zin! Zin! A Violin (Moss)
Moose on the Loose (Ochs)
Dinosaur Chase (Otto)
Pigs in the Mud in the Middle of the Rud (Plourde & Schoenherr)
My Parents Think I'm Sleeping (Prelutsky)
Down by the Bay (Raffi)
We're Going on a Bear Hunt (Rosen)
Frogs in Clogs (Samton)
A Twister of Twists, A Tangler of Tongues (Schwartz)
There's a Wocket in my Pocket (Seuss)
Sheep on a Ship (Shaw)
The Listening Walk (Showers)
Eight Ate: A Feast of Homonym Riddles (Terban)
The Lady with the Alligator Purse (Westcott)

Figure 4.2. Children's Books for Phonological Awareness.

PHONEMIC AWARENESS PROGRAMS (COMMERCIALLY AVAILABLE)

- Fundations
- Ladders to Literacy
- Lindamood Phoneme Sequencing
- Open Court
- Phonemic Awareness in Young Children: A Classroom Curriculum
- Phonological Awareness Training for Reading
- Road to the Code: A Phonological Awareness Program for Young Children
- Sounds Abound

ASSESSING PHONEMIC AWARENESS: INFORMAL MEASURES

1) Rhyming (To avoid any confusion the term rhyme should be avoided when assessing a young child.)

Practice script:

"Some words end the same way. Listen as I say these words: *bat, cat, fat, hat.* These words all end in *at.* Now listen to these words: *got, man, car.* These words do not end the same way."

"Here are two more words: *man, fan.* Do they end the same way?" (If the student does not answer correctly, repeat the words and say, "They both end in *an.*")

Test script:

"I will say some words and you say *yes* if they end the same and *no* if they do not end the same."

(Score each item with a + for correct; or − for incorrect.)

> ball, fall _____   can, man _____
> wish, fish _____   bed, fun _____
> make, car _____   sing, wing _____
> bee, hit _____   say, may _____
> Score _____ / out of 8

Assessing Phonemic Awareness: Initial Phonemes

2) Isolating the first phoneme in one-syllable words beginning with continuous sounds.

Practice Script:

"Listen to the sound at the beginning of *sit*. Sit begins with /s/. What is the sound at the beginning of sit?" If the student answers correctly, continue, if not, say, "The sound at the beginning of *sit* is /s/. Say /s/."

Test Script:

"I will say a word and you say the sound at the beginning of the word."

(Score with a + or – for each item.)

> fan _____   lake _____
> map _____   not _____
> ride _____   sun _____
> van _____   zip _____
> Score _____ / out of 8

Assessing Phonemic Awareness: Final Phonemes

3) Isolating the last phoneme in a one-syllable word.

Practice Script:

"Listen to the sound at the end of the word *fan*. *Fan* ends with /*n*/. What is the sound at the end of *fan?*" If the student answers correctly, continue, if not, say, "The sound at the end of *fan* is /*n*/. Say /*n*/."

Test Script:

"I will say a word and you say the sound at the end of the word."

(Score with + or – for each item.)

➢	will _____	cab _____
➢	bat _____	bag _____
➢	cup _____	sad _____
➢	day _____	bake _____
➢	Score _____ / out of 8	

Assessing Phonemic Awareness: Phoneme Blending

4) Phoneme manipulation (blending):

Blending is putting together speech sounds (in proper sequence) to produce a word.
Practice Script:

"I am going to say the sounds in a word. Listen to the sounds and tell me the word they make. Let's do one together; /d/ /o/ /g/ makes what word? *Dog, that's correct.* Now, let's do a few more."

Test Script:

"I am going to say the sounds in a word. Listen to the sounds and tell me the word they make."

(Enter a + if the student says the word correctly; if not, write the student's response)

	Sounds (phonemes)	Word	Response
➢	/s/ /ē/ /d/	seed	_____

➢	/f/ /a/ /t/	fat	_____
➢	/c/ /u/ /p/	cup	_____
➢	/s/ /t/ /o/ /p/	stop	_____
➢	/sh/ /ā/ /k/	shake	_____
➢	/m/ /ā/ /d/	made	_____
➢	/d/ /i/ /sh/	dish	_____
➢	/b/ /e/ /l/	bell	_____
➢	Score _____ / out of 8		

Assessing Phonemic Awareness: Phoneme Segmentation

5) Phoneme manipulation (segmenting)

Segmenting is discriminating the phonemes within a word and pronouncing them in the correct sequence (i.e., the reverse of blending.)
Practice Script:

"I am going to say a word. Listen and then tell me the sounds that make up that word. Let's do one together. In the word *cat,* the sounds are /k/ /a/ /t/.

Test Script:

"Let's do a few more. Listen to the word I say, then, tell me all the sounds in the word."

(Underline each separate sound said correctly; record the incorrect student responses)

	Word	Sounds (phonemes)	Response
➢	dog	/d/ /o/ /g/	_____
➢	made	/m/ /ā/ /d/	_____
➢	neat	/n/ /ē/ /t/	_____
➢	bone	/b/ /ō/ /n/	_____
➢	time	/t/ /ī/ /m/	_____
➢	fill	/f/ /i/ /l/	_____
➢	jet	/j/ /e/ /t/	_____
➢	cap	/k/ /a/ /p/	_____
➢	Score _____ / 8		

THE ALPHABETIC PRINCIPLE

In a very functional way, children make use of their growing understanding of the names of the letters of the alphabet and the sounds that are associated with those letters as they begin to read and write. This is called the alphabetic principle. Children begin to make sense of the sounds of spoken language and the symbols of written language. In other words, they understand that what they say can be written down—they begin to realize the connection between printed letters and their corresponding sounds. Mastery of this concept helps children as they progress in their abilities to read words encountered in print and spell words they want to use in their writing. In a very real sense, children begin to unlock the code.

According to the National Reading Panel (2000), letter-sound knowledge, or understanding the alphabetic principle, is a prerequisite skill for effective word identification. As children develop their alphabet knowledge, they progress along a continuum. First, they begin to understand that words are composed of a specific sequence of letters; then they associate a grapheme (letter) with a corresponding phoneme (sound); and then they are able to identify words in which letters represent their most common sounds.

Once children grasp the alphabetic principle, they can begin to use the code to independently translate a visual symbol (a letter) into a sound (i.e., they begin to decode a series of letters into sounds that make up printed words). This connection is known as phonics.

Two underlying abilities, auditory discrimination and visual discrimination, are important to the formation of the mental connections between sounds and letters. Auditory discrimination is the ability to detect likenesses and differences in sounds (phonemes) heard, and visual discrimination is the ability to detect likenesses and differences in symbols (graphemes) viewed. Children should be provided with ample opportunities to practice these skills. Since letters that are very similar, either in the way they look or the way they sound, are apt to cause confusion, the sequence for introducing letters should take into account both visual similarity and auditory similarity (Carnine, et al., 2010). For example, because the letters *p* and *b* are visually similar except for their orientation in space, they may cause confusion. In addition to this fact, the *p* and the *b* have auditory similarity as well. That is, the /p/ is unvoiced and the /b/ is voiced. Practice saying these two sounds to demonstrate their similarity. In this case, there are two reasons they should not be introduced in the same lesson.

Recommendations for Developing Alphabetic Skills

- Read aloud to children and provide many alphabet books for exploration.
- Teach and sing the alphabet song and/or variations.
- Provide many opportunities to explore the alphabet tactually with manipulatives such as letter blocks, foam letter-shapes, and magnetic letters.
- Practice saying and tracing the shapes of letters on surfaces with texture (such as fine sandpaper).
- Practice saying and writing letter names in sand, shaving cream, or pudding.
- Provide a large visually interesting display of the alphabet and use it often.
- Play board games to practice skills (concentration/memory or letter bingo).

PHONICS

The ability to understand and use sound-symbol correspondences to decode words is an essential word recognition strategy. Instruction in this area is often referred to as phonics and is part of a complete literacy program. Phonics instruction helps children use the systematic relationships between graphemes and phonemes to retrieve the pronunciation of an unknown sequence of letters or to spell words. Research suggests that there are long-term benefits when children develop an understanding of the alphabetic principle and are able to apply those skills in their reading and writing (Roberts, 2003; Solilty, Deavers, Kerfoot, Crane & Cannon, 1999). In order to teach children how to use the alphabetic principle, teachers must be fluent in all the essential elements. What follows is a list of essential phonics terms teachers should know and teach.

Essential Phonics Terms to know

1) Consonants: Letters other than *a, e, i, o, u*

- Consonant Blends or Clusters: 2 or more successive consonant letters blend together (Each consonant retains its own individual sound, e.g., *bl, st, dr*).
- Consonant Digraphs: 2 successive consonants that represent one speech sound. (*di* meaning 2; and *graph* meaning written symbol, e.g., *ch, th, sh*).
- Initial consonant: A consonant at the beginning of a syllable or word.
- Final Consonant: A consonant at the end of a syllable or word.

2) Decoding: The process of using letter-sound correspondences to recognize words.
3) Decodable Text: A selection or passage containing a majority of words that can be decoded or read using the most common sounds of the letters or letter-sound correspondences that have already been learned.
4) Grapheme: A written symbol that represents a phoneme.
5) Most Common Sound of a Letter: The sound a letter typically makes in a short, one-syllable word.
6) Phoneme: A single distinctive sound in the language.
7) Regular Words and Irregular Words: A regular word is made up of letters that represent each letter's most common sound, while an irregular word contains one or more letters in which the letter(s) does not represent its most common sound.
8) Sight words: Words that can be read automatically—they are known by sight (without vocalizing the individual sounds in a word).
9) Sounding out: The process of pronouncing each sound (represented by a letter or combination of letters) in a word.
10) Stop Sounds and Continuous Sounds: A stop sound can only be pronounced for an instant. A word beginning with a stop sound is more difficult for children to sound out, while a continuous sound can be held without distortion (emphasized) and is therefore, easier to sound out.
11) Syllable: A unit of spoken language (containing a vowel sound) that is next bigger than a speech sound (phoneme).
12) Vowels: Letters *a, e, i, o, u* (w and y in the final position of words or syllables; y in the medial position). The vowel is the one most prominent sound in a syllable.

- Diphthongs: Vowel sounds that are closely blended in a word and the position of the mouth changes from one place to another as the sound is produced (oil, boy, cow, out). The sound is usually not the short or long sound of the vowels in the pattern.
- R-controlled vowel: When a vowel or vowel digraph is combined with the consonant *r* the vowel sound is influenced (controlled) by the sound of the /r/.
- Short vowel: The pronunciation is shorter than the "long" vowel and does not sound like the letter's name.
- Single long vowel: The pronunciation sounds like the letter's name.
- Vowel Digraph: Two vowels or a vowel and silent consonant(s) that make one sound (typically the long or short vowel sound of one of the letters in the vowel combination).

The National Reading Panel (2000) reported that systematic phonics instruction contributed to overall progress in reading for children from all socioeconomic status backgrounds. Furthermore, the NRP (2000) reported that effective phonics instruction should enable children to do the following: Differentiate individual sounds within words; blend sounds to make words; use letter and sound correspondence to figure out new words; recognize and use patterns in words—first in one-syllable words and later in multi-syllable words. See Figure 4.3.

Furthermore, the panel concluded that effective phonics instruction should be linked to real reading activities so that children practice their newly learned skills in reading words and connected text. In addition, instruction should help children apply these skills to their spelling and writing. As with any area of instruction, phonics instruction should be based on assessment and adapted to the needs of individual students.

Children must practice their newly acquired skills in real world meaningful ways. The must read, read, read, and write, write, write! In order to become efficient and competent readers and writers, children must be given many opportunities to observe expert readers and writers and apply their developing literacy skills. As children gain experience with receptive written language (reading) and expressive written language (writing), they begin to understand the following written language concepts more deeply.

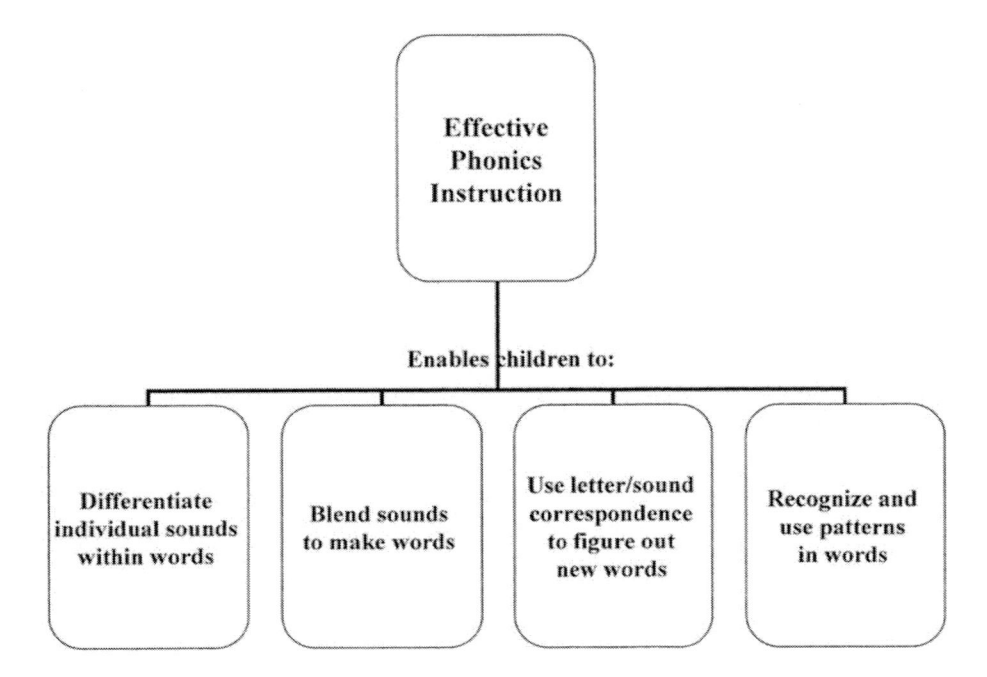

Figure 4.3. Effective Phonics Instruction.

Written Language Concepts

- What is spoken can be written down, and each individual speech sound can be represented by a letter or combination of letters.
- Words are read from left to right, and top to bottom on the page.
- Words are spelled from left to right.
- A letter's phoneme (sound) can be influenced by its position within a pattern.

    o   Mad, short *a* (CVC)
    o   Made, long *a* (CVCe)

- Some different letter patterns can represent the same sounds.

    o   Made, long *a* (CVCe)
    o   Mail, long *a* (CVVC)

- Some spelling patterns and corresponding sounds generalize across words (word families).

  - o   *ay*: bay, day, may, say, way
  - o   *igh*: high, sigh, light, flight

- Other spelling patterns have different sounds when in different words.

  - o   *ou*: about, bought, soul

Systematic exposure to the alphabetic principle through practice with real reading, in addition to direct instruction in the predictable patterns within words, helps children develop the literacy skills necessary to make predictions about new words they encounter in print or want to spell in their writing. It is important to remember that children attain literacy skills at different rates and need differing amounts of practice to master specific skills. Therefore, individual assessment and progress monitoring are vital to all components of a literacy program.

Tips for Teaching Phonics

First, it is important to build on what children already know about the alphabetic principle. When children have experience with books, magazines, computers, labels, signs, text messages, etc., they are better able to approach reading as a meaningful activity. In addition, making sure that reading is a fun activity for every child, no matter their level, is crucial. Every child should experience success—not at the same level or in the same time period—and it is the responsibility of teachers and families alike to provide each child with the opportunities and the tools for success. The following are some suggestions to keep in mind when teaching phonics:

1) Master the simple before proceeding to the more complex:

    - Begin with continuous sounds before stop sounds.
    - Introduce letters and sounds that can be easily differentiated (they are not similar in sound or appearance).
    - Introduce new letters in the initial position before the final position.

- Introduce words that have high utility in the child's reading.
- Introduce CVC pattern words before CCVC or CVCe pattern words.
- Introduce consistent patterns before variable patterns.
- Focus on onsets (the part of a syllable before the vowel) and rimes (includes the vowel to the end of the syllable).

2) Provide many opportunities for children to observe a model unlock/decode letter patterns and then practice these new skills with support.
3) Help students use new phonics knowledge to focus on reading words and stories.
4) Encourage children to experiment with sounds and letters in their writing (developmental spelling or invented spelling).
5) Encourage children to compare and contrast features of words.
6) Monitor progress in order to effectively plan future instruction.
7) Be responsive to individual student needs.

Remember that teaching children how to use phonics is one part of a much larger picture. It is a very useful tool in word recognition. However, phonics instruction should be employed with the end goal in mind. That is, the ultimate goal of all reading instruction is to help children develop the skills that will make them fluent and efficient consumers of text such that they are able to comprehend what they read. Phonics instruction should take place within the larger framework of a complete literacy program that utilizes real and purposeful reading.

Assessing the Alphabetic Principle and Phonics: Informal Measures

1) Correct identification of letter names in words:

Practice Script:

"Listen to the word *zebra*. Say *zebra*. What is the name of the first letter you hear in *zebra?* Yes, *z* is the name of the first letter in the word zebra."
Test Script:

"Let's do a few more. Listen to the word I say, then, tell me the name of the first letter you hear?"

(Enter a + for each correct letter; enter the incorrect letter name)

April ____		deep ____	
eat ____		idol ____	
over ____		peach ____	
team ____		unit ____	
Score ____ / 8			

Informal Assessment: Initial Single Consonant Sounds

2) Initial single consonant sounds:

Script:

"Look at these two letters. (Point to *at* on the test sheet.) They say *at*. If we add a letter to the beginning of *at* we make a new word or nonsense word. Read the list by adding the sound of the first letter to the middle letters *at*. Say the word or nonsense word."

Test items:
(Mark correct responses with +; record any incorrect sounds.)

b	at	bat ____		m	at	mat ____
c	at	cat ____		n	at	nat ____
d	at	dat ____		p	at	pat ____
f	at	fat ____		r	at	rat ____
g	at	gat ____		s	at	sat ____
h	at	hat ____		t	at	tat ____
j	at	jat ____		v	at	vat ____
k	at	kat ____		w	at	wat ____
l	at	lat ____		z	at	zat ____
Score ____ / out of 18						

Informal Assessment: Initial Consonant Blends

3) Initial consonant blends:

Script:

"Look at these two letters. (Point to *at*. They say *at*. If we add letters to the beginning of *at* we make a new word or nonsense word. Read the list by adding the sounds of the first letters to the middle letters *at*. Say the word or nonsense word.*"*

Test items:
(Mark correct responses with +; record any incorrect sounds.)

bl	at	blat	_____
sk	at	skat	_____
br	at	brat	_____
sl	at	slat	_____
cl	at	clat	_____
sm	at	smat	_____
cr	at	crat	_____
sn	at	snat	_____
dr	at	drat	_____
sp	at	spat	_____
fr	at	frat	_____
st	at	stat	_____
fl	at	flat	_____
sw	at	swat	_____
gl	at	glat	_____
tr	at	trat	_____
gr	at	grat	_____
scr	at	scrat	_____
pl	at	plat	_____
spr	at	sprat	_____
pr	at	prat	_____
str	at	strat	_____
sc	at	scat	_____

Score _____ / out of 23

Informal Assessment: Consonant Digraphs

4) Consonant Digraphs:

Script:

"Look at these two letters. (Point to *ot*. They say *ot*. If we add letters to the beginning of *ot* we make a new word or nonsense word. Read the list by adding the sound of the first letters to the middle letters *ot*. Say the word or nonsense word."

Test items:

sh ot	shot	_____
ch ot	chot	_____
ph ot	phot	_____
th ot	thot	_____
wh ot	whot	_____

Score _____ / out of 5

Informal Assessment: Vowels

5) Vowels:

Script:

"Here are some more words and nonsense words. Do your best to read them."

(Mark correct items with +; write incorrect responses.)

Short vowels		Long vowels (silent *e*)		Long vowel pairs	
pap	_____	pite	_____	peem	_____
pep	_____	pote	_____	paim	_____
pip	_____	pute	_____	poam	_____
pop	_____	pate	_____	peam	_____
pup	_____	pete	_____		

Score _____ / out of 14

QUESTIONS FOR REFLECTION AND DISCUSSION

1) How did you learn to read? Did you remember receiving instruction in phonics?
2) Describe what you remember about your early reading instructional experiences.
3) How comfortable are you with the essential elements of phonics? Why do you feel this way? If your skills are not up to what they should be in order for you to teach phonics, what do you need to do to improve your skills in this area?

CHAPTER APPLICATION EXERCISES

1) Design a scripted lesson plan for teaching phonemic awareness skills. Write what the teacher will say and write the children's expected responses.
2) Design a hands-on activity/game for practicing phonemic awareness skills.
3) Perform a read-aloud with a children's book that plays with language.
4) Keep in mind the visual and auditory similarity of the letters. Then create an acceptable sequence for introducing the letters and their sound correspondences.
5) Create a scripted lesson plan for teaching children to decode simple CVC words. Assume the children already know the common sounds for letters *m, s, t, c, d, a, i, o*. Be very specific. Write what the teacher will say and the expected responses from the children.
6) List the following words from easiest to decode to most difficult to decode. Explain your reasoning. *Fast, black, man, slim, city, cat*

Chapter 5

WORD RECOGNITION AND WORD ANALYSIS

"A word is not a crystal, transparent and unchanged. It is the skin of a living
thought and may vary greatly in color and content according to the
circumstances and the time in which it is used."
(Justice Oliver Wendell Homes)

Word recognition should be taught within the context of real reading activities that are meaningful to the child with automaticity as the goal. Automaticity is the term used to indicate a reader is able to recognize words with ease (automatically), whereby the amount of working memory capacity used in the act of reading is relatively small. This leaves more processing capacity for comprehension. On the other hand, when a reader struggles with word recognition, so much effort may be expended in the slow and sometimes intensive process that comprehension of the material may be almost nonexistent (Just & Carpenter, 1992; LaBerge & Samuels, 1974). This is typical of beginning readers and of older struggling readers.

It is essential that beginning reading instruction include opportunities for developing automaticity in word recognition. Phonics instruction is one of the foundation or building blocks. There are five methods that readers use to use to identify words and they include the following: prediction, sounding out, chunking, reading by analogy, and immediate recognition (Gunning, 2010). Of these methods, obviously immediate recognition is the most efficient. With this in mind, since there are certain words that occur with high frequency in children's literature, it makes sense to focus instructional attention on these words.

AUTOMATICITY

Reading, reading, and more reading promotes automatic word recognition. In other words, concentrated practice reading high frequency words in their natural context (in connected text) is perhaps the best way to achieve automaticity. The opposite of automatic word recognition is word-by-word reading where children are so focused on decoding each letter-sound that the process is very slow and methodical. Fluency, or the flow and rhythm of reading, is disrupted, and deficits in comprehension often follow.

Decodable texts are texts that emphasize words that have been the focus of phonics instruction and have already been mastered by the individual children using them. They are used to reinforce phonics elements and are a stepping-stone to other forms of children's literature. Although the term decodable text is used to describe a reading selection or story, in reality no text is completely decodable. Some words will have to be taught as sight words. There are two primary reasons for this. First, there are some frequently occurring words in English that do not follow the typical phoneme-grapheme correspondence. In addition, in order for a story or selection to maintain cohesion and interest, some words that contain letter-patterns not yet learned will most likely be included in a given text. In fact, one criticism of decodable texts is that they often sound contrived or unnatural due to the effort to include only decodable words. However, decodable texts are a good way to practice newly learned skills in a real reading setting until children are equipped with the necessary skills to move on to other forms of children's literature. Beginning reading materials are often leveled based on the key elements (short vowels, long vowels, clusters, vowel digraphs, etc.) they contain. Care should be exercised to make sure that children are matched with an appropriate level text

At this point, emphasis on children's writing can be used to reinforce phonics and word recognition skills. Encouraging children to use developmental (invented) spelling can help reinforce phonics skills they are using in their reading. As children progress in their ability to express themselves they move from drawings to symbol-like line forms (prephonemic), to alphabetic and orthographic invented spelling (phonemic), and finally toward conventional spelling. Language-experience stories can be beneficial for both reading and writing skill development. The language-experience approach (LEA) can be an individual activity or shared writing activity that incorporates reading, writing, speaking, and listening. In this approach children write or dictate stories to a teacher or other capable writer. Then the passage is used for reading instruction. In this way children learn about literacy connections in a concrete manner.

Structural analysis of words (syllabication) is another important strategy for word recognition, and it involves the recognition of letter patterns, prefixes, roots, and suffixes. Structural analysis is also referred to as morphology, because it involves the study of meaning-bearing units. Instruction should be explicit and systematic, and then additional practice should take place within the context of real and meaningful reading. Although many of the most frequent words children will encounter in their beginning reading have a single syllable, by second grade it is estimated that more than 30 percent are multisyllabic (Gunning, 2010). The need for instruction is clear, and as always the purpose of the instruction is to help children develop the skills necessary to comprehend what they read. Word study activities should be enjoyable and reinforce instruction. Children should be given substantial amounts of meaningful reading so they are repeatedly exposed to and are able to examine many words. This builds their sight word vocabularies. Classroom displays such as word walls—a visual display and reminder of word study properties—may be posted for handy reference and prompts. In addition, systematic review and rehearsal of known words, along with the systematic addition of new words with rehearsal until mastery is achieved, will help children retain what they learn. Simple word-card games and board games may be used to reinforce specific skills (word sorts, bingo, concentration, modified scrabble game, etc.), and word-part manipulation (a felt board with felt letters and word parts) may be used to form word families and reinforce patterns. As illustrated in Figure 5.1, these activities work together to reinforce word learning.

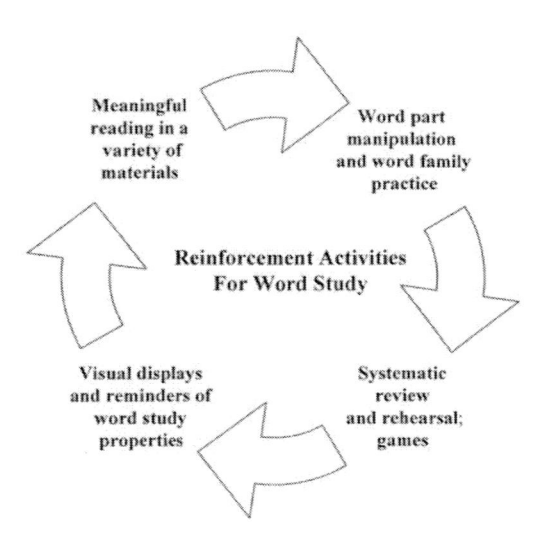

Figure 5.1. Reinforcement Activities for Word Study.

In working on word recognition skills teachers should keep the following in mind:

- Practice should incorporate a review of previously learned skills and reinforcement of newly learned skills.
- Help children make connections.
- Keep the end goal in mind (comprehension).
- Make instruction systematic.
- Reading materials should be easy (but not too easy). Individual reading levels should be based on progress monitoring (on-going assessment).
- Children need to practice skills within the context of real reading
- Encourage independence (reading lots of books at the child's independent level supports and promotes automatic and fluent word recognition).
- Insure opportunities for success to build motivation and the child's reading self-efficacy.
- Small-group (or one-to-one) instruction allows for close monitoring of progress.

Since automaticity is the immediate processing of information and is important in reading skill development, it follows that when word or phrase recognition is automatic, cognitive effort may be directed toward comprehension of the text. On the other hand, effortful processing of words and phrases may require considerable focus and effort. That is, when word recognition is effortful (not automatic) additional processing is needed in order for accurate word and phrase recognition to occur. Theory has long held that automatization failure causes an individual to allocate attention and exert effort that they would not otherwise have to do (Just & Carpenter, 1992; LaBerge & Samuels, 1974). The need for systematic and continued practice over time is evident, in particular for those children who demonstrate weaknesses in the area of automatic word recognition.

MORPHOLOGICAL AWARENESS

Morphological awareness is the ability to use the smallest meaning units of language (morphemes) to speak, understand, read, and spell words. Morphology, the study of the structure of words, includes patterns of derivation, inflection, and compounding. Derivation involves forming words from other words or basic forms with the use of affixes (e.g., joy + ful). Inflection involves a change in a word's form or function with the addition of a suffix (e.g., plural markers, verb endings, possessives, and comparative markers). For example, in English an s added to the end of the word *boy* changes the number (boy + s means more than one boy); an *ed* added to the end of the word *play* changes the tense (play + ed signifies past tense); an *'s* added to the end of a word signifies possession (*girl* + *'s* means belonging to the girl); and *er* or *est* added to the end of a word signals a comparison (*fast* + *est*). Compounding involves forming a new word by combining two whole words (e.g., *butter* + *fly*).

Generally, the first morphemes children use regularly in their speech include the plural marker *s* (e.g., The horses run), the possessive marker *'s* (e.g., The boy's hat), and the progressive ending *ing* (e.g., The dog's barking) (Gillam & Bedore, 2000). During this period, children demonstrate their overgeneralization of the new rules when they use *mouses* instead of *mice*. As children progress in their development of language skills and are exposed to words in oral language and in print they become more aware of the structure of words. However, students with disabilities often struggle with morphological forms such as the exceptions to tense markers (e.g., run—ran), or plurals (e.g., goose—geese).

In recent years, morphological instruction has received increased attention as a way to improve literacy achievement for children who struggle with reading and spelling (e.g., Reed, 2008; Siegel, 2008). Morphological awareness is a word analysis skill and is elemental to word identification accuracy, especially as children progress to more and more complex words. Moreover, a synthesis of the research in morphological instruction suggests that morphological instruction can improve both phonological as well as morphological awareness (Goodwin & Ahn, 2010).

Morphemes can be categorized as either free or bound. This distinction is made based on whether or not the morpheme is a word in and of itself (free morpheme), or whether the morpheme must be combined with other morphemes to form a word (bound morpheme). Free morphemes are words that have the role of carrying the meaning of the sentence (content) or of performing a function in a sentence (e.g., prepositions, pronouns, articles, conjunctions). On the other hand, bound morphemes include inflectional endings and affixes and must be combined with a free morpheme.

Teaching children to examine the structure of words and their meaningful parts is important to their reading independence. When children are taught to recognize the meaningful parts of words, unknown words encountered during independent reading may be decoded and understood when the word parts are familiar. On the other hand, due to the complex nature of the morphological structure of English, children with language development issues are likely to demonstrate difficulties with suffixes resulting in miscues in reading and misspellings in writing (e.g., *city's* or *citys*, instead of *cities*). Recent research examining the impact of morphological interventions on other reading skills demonstrated improvements in student vocabulary as well as in reading comprehension (Goodwin & Ahn, 2010). This finding is important particularly for students who struggle with literacy. Goodwin and Ahn (2010) suggest that instruction that helps students with literacy challenges identify morphemes and connect morpheme meanings within whole words supports word-meaning learning. Furthermore, students with literacy challenges also benefit from practice with word families. This promotes awareness of the relationship between words and is thought to help lexical access—the retrieval of words that are connected in meaning (Nagy, Anderson, Schommer, Scott, & Stallman, 1989).

Moats (2010) suggests the following,

> …we typically expect children to gain and use knowledge of inflectional and derivational morphology without explicit instruction or we teach them about word parts in a cursory way … Word structure at the morpheme level, however, should begin in the first grade. All children can benefit from understanding how their language works, but children who have deficits in linguistic awareness really need explicit, systematic, and direct instruction with ample practice opportunities. (p. 143)

For young children informal measures of morphology may provide valuable information regarding their mastery of correct morphological forms. For example, to explore receptive morphology the child may be asked to point to a picture that illustrates a morpheme. To examine expressive morphology the child may be presented with a series of pictures depicting actions such as walking, swimming, running, or jumping, and asked to tell the teacher what the person in the picture is doing. The need for instruction is indicated if the child is not able to respond with the expected form (e.g., The boy is *jumping*.)

Instruction in morphology should begin with the introduction of forms that are obvious; forms that are most commonly used; and forms that do not involve orthographic (spelling) or phonological (pronunciation) challenges. In addition, instruction should be provided in an explicit and systematic manner. This gives children a reliable structure to begin to learn about the morphology of the English language. In addition, beginning instruction should include the formation and use of noun plurals; noun possessives; third person singular of present tense verbs; past tense of regular and irregular verbs; comparative and superlative forms of adjectives; inflectional endings; noun derivation; adverb derivation; and prefixes.

Morphological Awareness Activities for Young Children (Small Groups)

- To teach noun plurals:

    o   The teacher asks students to raise their finger puppet every time they hear a word that means more than one of something (e.g., *boy, boys, girl, girls, dog, dogs*).

    o   The teacher shows several picture cards that depict plural nouns and names each picture. The students repeat after the teacher. Then the teacher asks the students to respond to several new pictures. When the students correctly respond to the new pictures, 10 new pictures are presented and the students are asked to name them.

- To teach noun possessives:

    o   Use two stacks of picture cards (one containing people, animals, etc., and the other containing items that could belong or be related to the first stack). The teacher holds up two cards and names the relationship (e.g., the girl's book, the boy's pencil). The students repeat after the teacher. Then the students are asked to respond to several new pairings.

- To teach past tense of verbs:

    o   Use puppets to demonstrate actions. For example the teacher demonstrates the action with the puppet and says, "He is hopping," Then the teacher says "He hopped very high." The students repeat after the teacher, and then produce the past tense forms on their own. Once regular verb forms have been mastered, this activity may be used to teach irregular past tense verb forms (e.g., ate, rode). Music may be added.

Elementary Level Students: Suggestions for Morphological Awareness

- Teach syllable awareness. Pronounce words one at a time and ask, "How many syllables are there? If I take off the last syllable, what is left? Is it a word you know?" (e.g., rainy; reading; stylish; biggest; happening; education)
- Practice identifying prefixes, roots, and suffixes by using a marker to color code.

Some suggestions for instructional mastery of morphological elements at the elementary level are presented in Table 5.1.

Table 5.1. Morphological Elements

Suggestions for Instructional Mastery of Morphological Elements:
Elementary Level

Common prefixes, meanings, and examples:	Common suffixes in nouns, meanings, and examples:	Common suffixes in verbs, meanings, and examples:
auto (self): automatic bi (twice): bicycle circum (around): circumstance con (with, together): congregate de (down, take away): deflate dis (away, apart): disadvantage im (not): immoral mis (wrong): misuse multi (many): multigrain pre (before): preview semi (partly, half): semicircle	ance, ence (state, act, fact): independence ation, ition, tion (action or state): saturation hood (condition): neighborhood ity, ty (quality): agility ment (result, action): pavement ness (quality): happiness	ate (cause to become): animate en (make or become): enliven fy (make or cause): beautify ize (cause to be): idealize

- Practice the schwa sound. That is, point out that vowels lose their distinct sound when they are in an unaccented syllable. Have students practice by saying CVC pattern words and non-words and then saying those same CVC patterns in an unaccented syllable (e.g., ton and carton; pet and carpet; gel and angel).
- Construct a word wheel to practice word building with a root word. Cut two circles the same size from a piece of cardstock. On one

circle write the appropriate prefixes at the outside edge. Cut a window in the other circle. Attach the two cardboard circles together (the circle with the window on top) with a brad. Place the root words on the top circle so that when the wheel is rotated the window with the prefixes will be adjacent to the root words (e.g., in-tend; ex-tend; pre-tend). Have students determine whether or not the combinations are real words.

- Have students create graphic organizers to show how word families are formed from a root word.

English Orthography

Orthography is the written system of a language. English orthography incorporates both phoneme—grapheme correspondences and morphology. English spellings are influenced by such things as word history (derivation), sound patterns, and spelling conventions, and morphology. Undoubtedly, spelling is an important skill in written expression, and there are many tools available to help writers spell words correctly. For instance, word processing programs have spell-checking capabilities. In addition, reference books such as dictionaries are frequently used as spelling aids.

Also, children should be made aware of some general spelling rules. However, it should also be pointed out that there are exceptions to the rules.

General Spelling Rules

1) *ie* and *ei:* Traditional rhyme: "*I* before *e*, except after *c,* or sounding as *a* in neighbor and weigh":

   a) write *ie* when the vowel sound is the *long e* (except after *c*):

   Examples: belief, field, relief; ceiling, deceive
   Exceptions to the rule: neither, leisure, seize, weird

   b) Write *ei* when the vowel sound is not the *long e* sound, especially when the sound is the *long a* sound:

   Examples: reign, weight, eight, freight, neighbor, height.

Exceptions to the rule: friend, mischief.

2) -sede, -ceed, -cede:

Only one word ends in *sede* (supersede).
Only three words end in *ceed* (exceed, proceed, succeed).
Other words with the similar sound end in *cede* (concede, precede, recede).

3) Prefixes: One or more letters are added to the beginning of a root word to change its meaning.

(Adding a prefix does not change the spelling of the word)

Examples: dis + trust = distrust; il + logical = illogical; im + moral = immoral; in + attentive = inattentive; mis + use = misuse; non + compliant = noncompliant; over + see = oversee; pre + view = preview; re + turn = return; sub + marine = submarine; un + able = unable.

4) Suffixes: One or more letters added to the end of a root word to change its meaning or its usage (part of speech).

a) When *–ness* and *–ly* are added, the spelling of the word usually stays the same:

Examples: Careful + ly = carefully, casual + ly = casually, great + ness = greatness, quick + ness = quickness; shy + ness = shyness.

Exceptions: Words ending in *y* (of more than one syllable), usually change the *y* to *i* before *ness* and *ly* (e.g., happy + ness = happiness; happy + ly = happily).

b) When adding a suffix which begins with a vowel (e.g., able, al, ing), drop the final *e* of the word:

Examples: remove + able = removable, approve + al = approval, confine + ing = confining

c) If the suffix begins with a consonant (e.g., less, ment, ful) keep the final *e:*

   Examples: care + less = careless, pave + ment = pavement, care + ful = careful

d) Words ending in *consonant + y (Cy)*—change the *y* to *i* (except suffixes beginning with *i*):

   Examples: Try + ed = tried, cry + ed = cried, bury + al = burial

e) Suffixes beginning with *i:*

   Examples: Cry + ing = crying, fly + ing = flying

f) Words ending in *vowel + y (Vy)*—generally do not change spelling:

   Examples: pay + ing = paying, stay + ing = staying

g) One syllable words ending in single VC—double the consonant before adding *ing, ed, er:*

   Examples: Sit + ing = sitting, stop + ed = stopped, trim + ing = trimming, run + er = runner

h) Two or more syllable words ending in single VC—double the consonant if the word is accented on the last syllable:

   Examples: concur + ed = concurred, begin + ing = beginning, begin + er = beginner

   If the word is NOT accented on the last syllable, do not double the final consonant:
   Examples: cancel + ed = canceled, travel + er = traveler, marvel + ing = marveling

i) Regular Plural Nouns (adding *s and es*):

j) In general, add *s* to the end of a noun to indicate the plural form:

Examples: chairs, colleges, dogs, thoughts

k) Some nouns ending in *s, x, z, ch, sh*—add *es* to the end of the word:

Examples: dresses, boxes, churches, wishes

l) Nouns ending in *Cy*—change the *y to i* and add *es:*

Examples: university, universities; pansy, pansies; city, cities

m) Nouns ending in *Vy*—add *s:*

Examples: day, days; ski, skis; journey, journeys

n) Generally--nouns ending in *f or fe*—add *s:*

Examples: belief, beliefs; gaffe, gaffes

o) Sometimes--nouns ending in *f or fe*—change *f to v* and add *s or es:*

Examples: knife, knives; shelf, shelves; calf, calves; wife, wives

p) Nouns ending in *Vo*—add *s:*

Examples: patio, patios; radio, radios

q) Nouns ending in *Co*—add *es:*

Examples: tomato, tomatoes; echo, echoes

5) Irregular plural nouns:

a) Sometimes the spelling of the word changes:
Examples: child, children; man, men; woman, women; foot, feet; mouse, mice; goose, geese; ox, oxen; tooth, teeth

b) Sometimes the spelling remains the same in singular and plural form:

Examples: deer, deer; moose, moose; salmon, salmon; sheep, sheep

c) Compound nouns (noun + modifier) – make the noun plural:

Examples: sister-in-law, sisters-in-law; passerby, passersby

6) Words often mistakenly used or spelled: Pronunciation and spelling is similar:

a) Accept and except:

Accept: to receive with consent; to give approval to
Except: to leave out; with the exclusion of; but

b) Affect and effect:

Affect: to influence; to produce an effect upon
Effect: the result of an action; a consequence

c) Capital and capitol:

Capital: the seat of government, a city; an uppercase letter
Capitol: The building (capitalized)

d) Course and coarse:

Course: path of action, planned program
Coarse: crude, rough

e) Council and counsel:

Council: a group of people who meet together
Counsel: to give advice

f) Desert, desert, dessert:

Desert: a dry sandy region
Desert: to leave or abandon
Dessert: the final course of a meal

g) Hear, here:

Hear: to perceive through the auditory senses
Here: in this place, location

h) Its and it's:

Its: possessive pronoun
It's: contraction of *it is, it was*

i) Plane, plain:

Plane: airplane, a flat surface in geometry, a carpentry tool
Plain: common, ordinary or unadorned; a flat area of land

j) Principal and principle:

Principal: the head of a school; main or most important something
Principle: a rule of conduct; a main fact or law

k) Shone and shown:

Shone: (the past tense of shine)
Shown: (the past tense of show)

l) Than and then:

Than: a conjunction used to compare something
Then: at that time

m) There, their, they're:
There: in a location, place; or to begin a sentence
Their: plural possessive pronoun
They're: contraction of *they are*

n) Threw and through:

Threw: hurled (past tense of throw)
Through: a preposition indicating a relationship

o) To, too, and two:

To: a preposition (I went to Los Angeles for a visit); used with a verb (I want to become an excellent writer)
Too: also; more than enough
Two: the number

p) Weak and week:

Weak: feeble; not strong
Week: 7 days

q) Weather and whether:

Weather: meteorology
Whether: a conjunction (The principal is wondering whether the students will enjoy the new playground setup.)

r) Who's and whose:

Who's: conjunction of *who is*
Whose: possessive

s) Your and you're:

Your: possessive
You're: conjunction of *you are*

QUESTIONS FOR REFLECTION AND DISCUSSION

1) How can teachers teach and reinforce word recognition and word analysis in grades one through three?

2) What is morphological awareness, and why is it important in the development of efficient literacy skills?
3) How are morphology and grammar related?

CHAPTER APPLICATION EXERCISES

1) Create a brochure summarizing important concepts from the chapter that could be shared with parents. Present the brochure to a local parent group.
2) Design a lesson plan to teach morphological awareness skills. Be sure the lesson includes modeling, guided practice, teacher/student interaction, student/student interaction, and rich language and literature examples.
3) Create an activity or game to reinforce morphological awareness for young children. Include directions for creating the activity and for playing the game with children.

Chapter 6

VOCABULARY AND FLUENCY

"I had fallen in love with words. What mattered was the sound of them as I
heard them for the first time…"
(Dylan Thomas)

VOCABULARY

Vocabulary involves two complementary word knowledge processes and is defined as the ability to understand (a receptive process) and use words (an expressive process). The overwhelming majority of learning, especially academic learning such as learning to read and write, is language based. Therefore, vocabulary knowledge is critical. Receptive vocabulary requires that children understand the meaning of given words through listening or reading, while expressive vocabulary requires that children understand and use specific words for meaning in speaking or writing. While children come to school with varying levels of vocabulary knowledge, children generally come to school understanding more words than they can use. That is, children's receptive vocabulary is larger than their expressive vocabulary. However, vocabulary instruction should be designed to increase both. In order for children to be successful in school, they must understand the vocabulary used by the teachers in the classroom for a variety of daily activities including following directions, understanding demonstrations, and learning classroom rules. Similarly, reading comprehension success requires that students understand the words they encounter in print.

Children learn many words through oral communications with adults and other children, listening to stories read to them, and through independent reading. However, the value of direct instruction should not be underestimated, because vocabulary development may be particularly challenging for students with disabilities. Early systematic and explicit vocabulary instruction can improve vocabulary development for young children who come to preschool and kindergarten with below level skills (Carnine, Silbert, Kame'enui, & Tarver, 2010).

One of the best ways for teachers and parents to encourage vocabulary development, and language development in general, is to model an appreciation of words and language through reading to children, talking with children, listening to children, and demonstrating a general love of words through a variety of oral language experiences.

There are several key ideas to keep in mind when planning vocabulary instruction for young children or children with disabilities. As illustrated in figure 6.1, reading to children regularly tops the list. When teachers have a sincere love of books and reading they make read-alouds a favorite part of the school day.

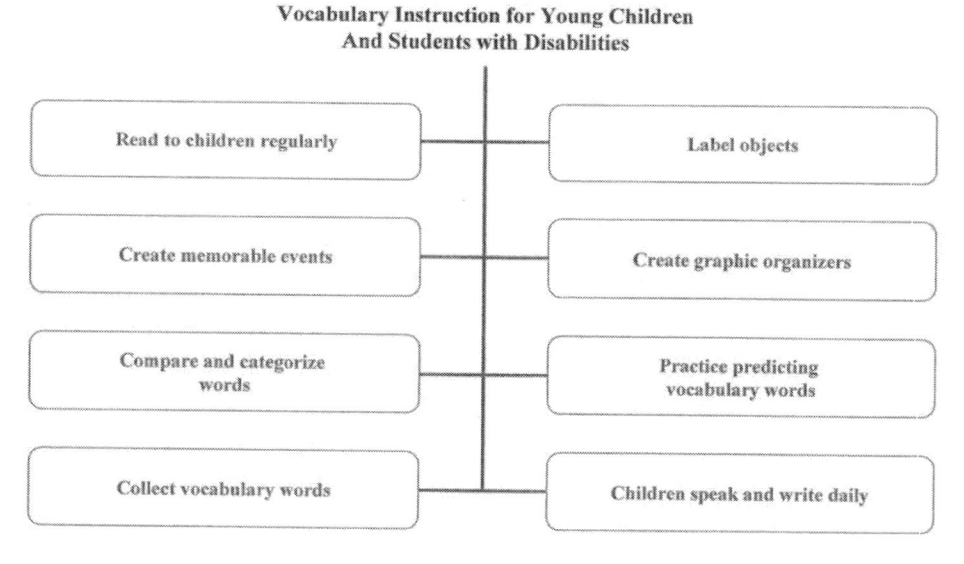

Vocabulary Instruction for Young Children And Students with Disabilities

Read to children regularly

Label objects

Create memorable events

Create graphic organizers

Compare and categorize words

Practice predicting vocabulary words

Collect vocabulary words

Children speak and write daily

Figure 6.1. Key Ideas for Vocabulary Instruction.

Another way to create an interest in words is to label objects around the classroom so that as children view an object they associate the label or print representation with the object. Other ways to improve vocabulary learning and retention are to create memorable events to spark retrieval of words and meanings; create graphic organizers for a visual representation of relationships; compare and categorize words based on features (use word sorts); provide opportunities for predicting vocabulary words; help children establish self-collection routines for vocabulary words; and finally provide abundant opportunities for children to speak and write within a safe, warm, and encouraging community of learners.

As children acquire reading skills, they also learn to read words already in their oral language vocabulary; learn to read and associate new words with concepts they already understand; and learn to read and understand new words for new concepts. Of these tasks, learning new words at the same time they are learning new concepts is the most difficult. Due to the fact that the meaning of words is often determined by the context in which they are used, hearing a word explained in context can be a helpful technique in vocabulary instruction. Understanding the meaning of individual words (vocabulary) is one of the key subskills involved in reading comprehension. Research suggests that direct instruction in vocabulary skills has a positive impact on both vocabulary and on reading comprehension for students with reading difficulties (Ebbers & Denton, 2008).

Shanker and Cockrum (2010, p. 147) suggest the following five progressive levels of vocabulary knowledge.

1) The child has no recognition of a word—may never have encountered the word before.
2) The child has heard of the word—but has no knowledge of the meaning.
3) The child recognizes the word in context and has a vague understanding of the meaning.
4) The child knows the word's meaning in the context in which it appears.
5) The child knows the multiple meanings of the word (if any) and can accurately use the word in thinking, speaking, or writing.

The need for vocabulary instruction continues as children progress through the grade levels, because the vocabulary demands, both in textbooks and academic language in general, steadily increases. This makes it imperative that vocabulary instruction address the needs of all students. Research indicates the time children spend in actual reading and their vocabulary growth rates are correlated. That is, extra time invested in reading is related to higher rates of vocabulary growth. For example, Anderson and Nagy (1993) conclude that the best way to foster vocabulary growth is to promote wide reading, because increased time spent in reading has a positive impact on fluency, knowledge of words and structures, and a broadened exposure to children's literature. "We advocate vocabulary instruction that promotes word consciousness, as sense of curiosity about word meanings, appreciation of nuances of meaning, and independence in word analysis." (Anderson & Nagy, 1993, p. 15)

There are several guiding principles teachers should follow in an effort to help children develop vocabulary. First, teachers are responsible for providing an environment conducive for vocabulary growth. In order to provide such an environment there are several things teachers can and should do. First of all, teachers should provide children with daily opportunities for wide reading, opportunities to build background knowledge, and multiple exposures to words, both orally and in print. Secondly, children need to be taught how and when to use strategies for learning new words. Next, teachers should scaffold learning such that they help children make connections (vocabulary to background knowledge), and help children see relationships between words and meanings. Finally, teachers must encourage an interest in words and make learning new words fun.

Another helpful component in teaching vocabulary is to teach word attack skills, specifically morphemic analysis. Morphemic analysis skills provide children with a way to examine word parts and their meanings. For example, the emphasis in morphemic analysis instruction is on words and their prefixes, suffixes, and roots. When children have morphemic analysis skills, they then have a strategy for exploring, learning, and adding new words to their vocabularies.

Contextual analysis is also an important strategy that children can be taught to use when learning new vocabulary words. Children may use context clues from the immediate sentence containing the unknown word, from text previously read, from picture clues, or examples and descriptions provided in the text. However, contextual analysis should be used in concert with other strategies and not relied on as the primary means to figure out words. Similar to other subskills that are foundational to skilled reading, children need to practice using context.

The use of scaffolding in instruction can provide the means for students to move along the path towards independent use of context. The process of scaffolding instruction means that a teacher, parent, or a more-skilled peer, provides assistance and guidance in learning so that children read and respond at a higher level than what they can currently do on their own. Scaffolding comes from the work of Vygotsky's theoretical model of learning and the concept of the Zone of Proximal Development (ZPD) (Vygotsky, 1978). For example, modeling how to figure out a word's meaning in the form of a think-aloud may be utilized at first to give children an expert example to imitate. Then the use of prompts and corrective feedback can be introduced and practiced with support. Finally, children should be encouraged to try using context clues on their own, while the teacher systematically monitors their progress.

Vocabulary development occurs along a continuum and is unique to each individual child. Children come to school with all sorts of experiences and circumstances which have an impact on their vocabulary development. In the beginning stages of reading, most children have all the words that they will encounter in print already in their vocabulary (at least receptive). However, this quickly changes as children progress in their reading levels, as well as in the grade levels. Children are progressively exposed to more and more new words, and many of the new words involve new concepts. It should also be noted that there is a wide range in the vocabulary levels of texts designed for young children.

Vocabulary instruction is a critical part of overall reading instruction. For young children, a good starting place for enhancing vocabulary development is to provide a variety of oral language experiences. One wonderful oral language opportunity for young children is listening to literature. When children are exposed to literature through read-alouds, for example, they hear words that they may not otherwise hear in their normal daily lives at home or in school. Their receptive vocabulary (listening) has the opportunity to dramatically increase, particularly when essential vocabulary words are introduced, discussed, defined, and processed prior to listening to the selection. Children are guided in their vocabulary acquisition by a more knowledgeable person (Vygotsky's ZPD), whether that person is a teacher, parent, sibling, or peer.

Although vocabulary development is typically thought of as being primarily a part of reading and language arts classes, vocabulary development is very much an integral part of other content areas such as science, mathematics, and social studies. Teachers must take care to model vocabulary acquisition techniques in these content areas as well as in the traditional language arts classes.

Techniques that require children to focus attention, actively work with words, work with words multiple times, and in different situations can have a positive impact on vocabulary development. For example, in one research study children learned approximately 40% more words when they processed the words at a deeper level by creating synonyms, antonyms, and graphic organizers for new words (Boulware-Gooden, Carreker, Thornhill, & Joshi, 2007). The children in the study were required to actually do something with the words and think about the words in several different ways, rather than simply rehearsing them or using them in a sentence. In addition, graphic organizers allow children to visualize concepts and their relationships to other already known concepts.

Classroom Vocabulary Activities

- Experiences: Provide experiences and then have follow-up discussions and/or debates. The experiences may include listening to stories and poems, listening to a guest speaker, viewing a film or video, going on a field trip.
- Word boxes: Have students create a word box with new words with child-friendly definitions related to their particular interests (e.g., ballet, music, dinosaurs) so they have ready access to vocabulary words in their writing.
- Shared interactive stories: Have students make up a shared story using newly learned vocabulary words. Each child takes a turn and contributes a sentence with a new word to the story. This may be completed either orally or in writing.
- Vocabulary Concept Circles: Circles are divided into parts (usually fourths) to provide a visual aid in determining relationships among words. This is a way to help with essential features and categorization skills.
- Semantic Maps (word maps/vocabulary maps): Students categorize words based on relationships in a visual manner with lines linking concepts. Semantic maps may include hierarchies and are often used with vocabulary in a content area such as science.
- Word Banks: As meanings are learned, vocabulary words are collected (usually on note cards). They may then be used in word sorts—categorization and classification based on similar features—as well in high interest word games.
- Synonym and antonym game: The class is divided into teams. When a team is presented with a vocabulary word they cooperate to come up with an appropriate synonym or antonym. Points are awarded for correct responses.
- Crossword puzzles with words that are related to a subject area: Students collaborate to complete the puzzle in small groups.
- Keyword strategy: The keyword strategy is a mnemonic device, and it links a new word or concept to a memorable image or keyword. Students may use the keyword strategy to illustrate words or new concepts in in a learning journal.

Making word learning fun and memorable can go a long way toward promoting vocabulary development. Using jokes, riddles, puns, silly rhymes, songs, and drama can create enjoyable ways to focus on vocabulary words. Vocabulary skills and strategies are critical to reading comprehension, because in order to understand the essence of a selection of text, children must understand the words that make up that selection. However, understanding the words is only part of the story of comprehension. Children must also have the appropriate background knowledge to make sense of a particular passage, understand text structures, and have reasoning and problem solving abilities.

Consider the following example. Examine whether or not the following words are in your own vocabulary: *assume, benefits, calculating, certainly, control, costs, eliminated, exceeded, extra, illustrate, impact, income, inventories, net, offset, purposes, savings, transfers, variances*. If so, does it follow that you will be able to comprehend a paragraph containing these vocabulary words? The answer is perhaps. Read the following from Ferrara, Dougherty, and Boer (1991).

However, even if one were to assume that the extra costs of calculating variances exceeded the savings created by ease in calculating transfers and inventories, the benefits of having variances for control purposes and to illustrate their impact on net income should certainly offset the extra cost of calculation. (p. 284)

In this case, the appropriate background knowledge (accounting) makes it much more likely that the reader will understand the passage.

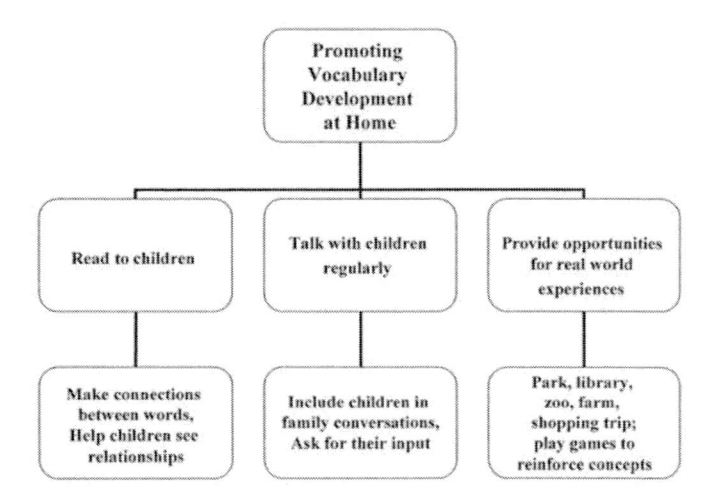

Figure 6.2. Promoting Vocabulary Development at Home.

Teachers should also encourage vocabulary development at home. The home-school bridge is an important one for children, and teachers can enlist the help of parents. Teachers can work with parents and encourage them and affirm their efforts (See figure 6.2). Teachers should encourage parents to talk with children regularly and encourage their questions; read to their children; include children in family conversations and ask for their input; offer child friendly description of word meanings; use visuals to help communicate meanings; make connections between words to help children see relationships; use games to reinforce concepts; and provide opportunities for real world experiences, such as going to the park, library, zoo, farm, or shopping.

FLUENCY

Another of the important components of efficient reading is fluency or the ability to read text in a smooth and flowing manner (both silently and orally). Fluent readers read with accuracy and attention to prosody. Prosody, the smooth rhythm of oral reading includes proper attention to pitch, intonation, stress, and timing. Fluent oral readers read with a rhythm and rate that is typical of oral language. They pause according to punctuation and apply emphasis to words and phrases accordingly. In the development of reading fluency, children learn to appropriately chunk words into meaningful units and phrases, and the ability to chunk words during reading is thought to be an indicator of comprehension (Kuhn & Stahl, 2003). Fluency and comprehension go hand-in-hand. In other words, when children develop fluency in reading, they are better able to comprehend what they read (Chard, Vaughn, & Tyler, 2002).

The underlying skills involved in automatic and accurate word recognition are essential to fluency and also to comprehension (Kuhn & Stahl, 2003). When children rely on sounding out too many words and word-by-word reading, reading rates tend to slow way down—fluency suffers. On the other hand, when children are able to read text with seemingly little cognitive energy expended, this allows the child to attend to and process the meaning of a given text. After all, the ultimate goal of all reading instruction is to help children develop the abilities that will allow them to comprehend (obtain meaning from) what they read.

Fluency rates should increase as children progress through the grade levels. The problem is that not all children develop adequate fluency. Research in the psychology of reading suggests that fluent word recognition within connected text is a prerequisite skill for good comprehension and enjoyable reading experiences (Nathan & Stanovich, 1991). The development of the essential underlying skills, and their working in concert, supports the process of reading—a psycholinguistic process in which the child constructs meaning from print (Harris & Sipay, 1990). Fluency is a reading skill that can be improved with practice and observation of (by listening to) proficient reading models. Fluency in reading connected text helps children grasp words and even phrases as whole units with immediate recognition, and this in turn contributes to faster reading rates. The development of fluency in reading also includes the ability to use prediction skills within sentence structures to help identify new words. According to Samuels (2006), the true test of fluency is to accurately and automatically read the words of a text, while simultaneously being able to comprehend the meaning. Furthermore, Rasinski (2006, p. 18) states that oral reading fluency "deals with reading words accurately and with appropriate speed, and it deals with embedding in one's voice elements of expression and phrasing while reading."

The Nature of Fluency Development

Fluency is a very complex process that requires interrelated skills to work in synchrony. Beginning readers (and older struggling readers) demonstrate a lack of fluency when they read slowly, haltingly, and with a lack of expression. A lack of fluency in reading can impact a child's confidence level, comprehension, and enjoyment of reading. Hence, fluency instruction and practice is critical and should be part of a balanced literacy program. According to Nathan and Stanovich (1991) not only is reading fluency important in cognitive theories of reading, it is also closely associated with reading comprehension, and is an overall indicator of reading efficiency. An alternative way to examine fluency is to monitor a student's rate of silent reading and compare their ability to answer comprehension questions. Gunning (2010) suggests that if students are able to answer comprehension questions correctly, and they finish a selection in a reasonable time, they probably have rapid and accurate word recognition. Carnine, Silbert, Kame'enui, and Tarver (2010) suggest that students' oral reading fluency should be monitored frequently, as often as weekly for those students who are performing below grade level, with sets of three one-minute oral reading assessments. They recommend the following target rates on the first one-minute oral reading (p.187):

- Grade One materials (2nd third)   45 words per minute (wpm)
- Grade One materials (last third)   60 wpm
- Grade Two materials (1st third)   75 wpm
- Grade Two materials (2nd third)   90 wpm

- Grade Two materials (last third)   110 wpm
- Grade Three materials (1ˢᵗ half)   120 wpm
- Grade Three materials (2ⁿᵈ half)   135 wpm
- Grade Four and above   150 wpm

The complex nature of reading fluency, as well as the relationship between reading fluency and reading comprehension, is interesting. The relationship is indeed so complex that some refer to comprehension in their explanation of what constitutes fluent reading. For example, Samuels (2002) suggests that a decisive test of reading fluency is the ability to simultaneously decode a text and comprehend the meaning. Fluent readers demonstrate the coordination of these abilities so that they are both accurate and fast in their ability to recognize words, and at the same time they use prosodic and syntactic knowledge to better comprehend text (Samuels, 2006).

Research studies document a relationship between reading fluency and comprehension. For instance, Reutzel and Hollingsworth (1993) reported that fluency training had a positive impact on second graders' reading comprehension, and more recently Pearce and Gayle (2009) found that oral reading fluency was a robust predictor of reading comprehension in third graders. According to Rasinski, Padak, and Fawcett (2010), reading fluency is a major concern for elementary level children and older children who have reading difficulties. In addition, they maintain that reading fluency instruction is essential, in particular for struggling readers, yet is an often underrepresented instructional goal for reading. Although the development of reading fluency is an essential skill for all children, children who demonstrate reading difficulties or who have learning disabilities need explicit fluency-based instruction (Algozzine, Marr, Kavel, & Dugan, 2009; National Reading Panel, 2000).

Consequently, a major instructional goal for beginning readers and struggling older readers is the transition from word-by-word, and often halting oral reading, to the smooth features inherent in fluent reading. Research suggests that when reading passages (selected for fluency instruction and practice) are closely aligned with children's instructional levels, children demonstrate gains in oral reading fluency measures (e.g., Martens, et al., 2007). Students need many opportunities to practice reading passages of connected text to reinforce both accuracy and fluency. This type of practice (at a child's instructional level—with approximately 95% accuracy or above) will encourage children to use their phonics skills to accurately recognize words that are new, and will also reinforce reading words previously learned to an automatic level. Automatic levels of word recognition promote fluency and comprehension. The following list includes some key ideas to keep in mind when selecting practice passages for fluency development.

Passages for Fluency Work

- Select passages that result in 95% or greater accuracy.
- Provide repeated opportunities for the child to practice the passages.
- Systematically increase criterion reading rate goals, while maintaining high accuracy levels. For example, maintain 97-98% accuracy as reading rates increase from 50 words per minute (wpm) to 60 wpm to 70 wpm, etc.
- As rates increase, begin to focus on reading with expression.

Building Fluency

There are many approaches that can be used to work on reading fluency (oral reading fluency in particular). Modeling is an integral part of all good instruction, and fluency instruction should begin with an explanation and modeling of appropriate rate and expression. This should be an extension of the read-alouds that have already been part of daily literacy activities in the primary classroom, with the process of reading aloud made even more explicit. Oral reading activities are vital to the development of reading fluency, and in order to monitor how children are progressing with fluency, teachers should use a small group instructional arrangement.

One method that encourages reading in phrases with attention to punctuation is the Neurological Impress Method (Heckleman, 1969). Passages are carefully selected with the intent that the less-skilled reader has at least 95% accuracy on word recognition for the words contained in the passages. This method is based on the theory that children will learn through the joint process of hearing their own voice, while listening to a proficient reader read passages of connected text. In this method, a skilled reader (teacher, parent, or peer) sits beside and slightly behind the child so that skilled reader's voice is directed into the child's ear. Fluent reading is modeled as the pair reads passages in unison. The skilled reader leads the reading and models appropriate changes in rate, emphasis, pausing, and intonation. In the beginning practice sessions, the skilled reader reads slightly louder and faster, and indicates place by sliding a finger smoothly along the words as they are read. When the child's fluency begins to improve, the skilled reader and the child may alternate roles as leader and follower.

Additional fluency building activities include shared or partner reading, choral reading, repeated reading, readers' theater, and tape recorded practice with passages. For example, the National Reading Panel (2000) concluded that repeated reading can positively impact reading fluency abilities of beginning readers. Repeated reading is exactly what the term implies. Children repeat the reading of a selection. This is done to promote automaticity and fluency. The same passage is read several times and both accuracy and reading rates are recorded. Repeated reading gives children the opportunity to become fluent with a passage. They know what words to expect and they have the opportunity to encounter the same words, phrases, and sentences over and over again.

For young children, shared reading (which may or may not include a big book) is a well-known reading activity that models fluent reading and begins to encourage beginning readers to imitate fluent reading characteristics. Often the teacher will introduce the reading selection by doing a picture walk. A picture walk is a visual survey of the illustrations of a story. As the teacher and children walk through the story together any important prior knowledge children need to understand the story can be discussed. In addition, children are often encouraged to make predictions about the characters, setting, storyline, ending, and so forth. The teacher may read part of the selection aloud and then have the children join in reading other parts in unison. Finally, children may be encouraged to read passages independently or with a partner (if the reading level is appropriate), and follow-up activities can be designed to provide additional modeling and instructional support as needed. Predictable books are a good choice for shared reading because they contain patterns or refrains that children love to join in and repeat over and over. For example, Mesmer (2010) found that reading fluency rates for first graders were enhanced within highly repetitive, predictable books that included high numbers of high frequency words.

Choral reading is another approach that builds fluency by having children read aloud together. There are variations of choral reading that suit different situations. For example, children may be divided into groups and then the groups read their own lines or paragraphs or parts together as a group, and the groups alternate or take turns reading their parts in unison. Another variation of choral reading may have a leader that reads parts of a selection, followed by the group unison response, much like readings in some church services. Choral reading is a flexible activity that can be used with a whole group or with small groups of children. One reason that it is a good way to encourage fluency development is that passages can be practiced with emphasis on different parts of oral reading fluency. That is, during one reading the focus may be on accuracy and rate, while during later readings the emphasis may be on expression, intonation and volume. Another advantage of choral reading in a group setting is that children who may not yet feel confident in their oral reading skills have a less intimidating way to practice these skills. In addition, children can listen to others (as a prosodic model) and hear their own voice (practice) at the same time.

Readers' theater is another fun-to-do activity that may be used to work on fluency. In readers' theater children dramatize a story by reading it aloud (much like a play, but not memorized). Each character, as well as the narrator, has lines that are read aloud to an audience. The readers rehearse their lines, plan a performance, and then carry out the performance for the audience of their choice (another class, parents, etc.).

Whisper reading is a fluency strategy that encourages children to read aloud, in a whisper, at their own rate. The teacher monitors individual children by moving around the room and listening as children read. A variation of whisper reading (also called echo reading) may be used in a one-to-one instructional setting where the teacher reads orally and the child whispers/echoes what is being read and is similar to the Neurological Impress Method described previously.

With each of these approaches to fluency development goals should be set and progress monitored systematically. While reading fluency goals must be realistic, they must also be challenging. Additionally, when planning fluency instruction, it is important to consider the child's interests, motivation, and self-efficacy for reading. Reading self-efficacy is the term used to describe how an individual feels about himself or herself as a reader. When teachers are familiar with children's interests they can provide a variety of reading materials so that children have a choice in what they read. Everyone likes to have a choice. Furthermore, children are more likely to be motivated to read when they have a say-so in what they read. According to Gambrell (1996) children with reading difficulties, as well as children who read well, are motivated by choice in reading material, shared oral reading, and affirmation of reading progress. Carnine, Silbert, Kame'enui, and Tarver (2010, p. 192) maintain,

Teachers have a responsibility to ensure that what occurs during instructional sessions will contribute to a child forming a positive self-image. The more success a child encounters during instruction, the more likely the instructional session will be a contributing factor for the development of a positive self-image.

In summary, to reach reading fluency goals children need to read often and widely so that they have meaningful practice with materials at their instructional and independent reading levels. Children need to have choices in what they read. They also need practice with frequently encountered sight words, as well as extensive practice in a variety of authentic oral reading activities. Finally, they need to see, hear, and emulate expert models of reading fluency.

QUESTIONS FOR REFLECTION AND DISCUSSION

1) Imagine you are working with a group of young children. Describe how you might teach the meaning of the following words: Between; false; opposite; damp

2) Think about some of your favorite children's books that are good examples of providing children with rich vocabulary. Give specific examples.

3) What are the characteristics of fluent reading? How does the term prosody fit in with the definition of fluency in reading?

4) Why is it important to teach fluency?

5) In your collaborative group generate several ways to have children participate in oral reading (without asking them to read in round robin fashion).

CHAPTER APPLICATION EXERCISES

1) In order to help children find excitement in learning new words, teachers must be enthusiastic word-connoisseurs. For the next few days, be aware of the new words you encounter. Write them down, and include the circumstances surrounding your experience with the new word. Be ready to enjoy your new words with others.

2) Plan a read-aloud for a group of children (ages 5 to 6). Select a book that you believe will provide a rich language experience. Create a lesson plan outline detailing how you plan to teach specific vocabulary contained in the selection.

3) Think about your personal philosophy of education. Then, consider which two of the suggested methods for improving reading fluency appeal to you the most? Write a one to two-page position paper defending your ideas.

Chapter 7

COMPREHENSION

"Knowledge itself is power."
(Francis Bacon, Lord Chancellor of England)

Reading comprehension is defined as the ability to bring meaning to what is read, and reading comprehension is the ultimate goal of the cumulative steps of all reading instruction. Reading comprehension involves three vital interactive factors: the reader, the text, and the purpose for reading. Therefore, the development of reading comprehension is a complex process and involves the subskills of phonemic awareness, alphabetic knowledge and phonics knowledge, fluency skills, vocabulary, background knowledge, reasoning abilities (including problem solving), text structure, and the purpose for reading (e.g., pleasure or information). Reading comprehension can be thought of as an evolving process that changes from the pre-reading stage to the during-reading stage to the post-reading stage (Roe, Smith, & Burns, 2009).

In large measure, reading comprehension has to do with factors unique to each individual reader, such as: background experiences, instructional experiences, interests, and facility with language. In the act of reading, in order to gain meaning, children must bridge the gap between the text and the background knowledge each uniquely brings to the task. Reading comprehension is an active process that depends on the interaction between the individual and text and is both intentional and thoughtful (National Reading Panel, 2000). Furthermore, Fraser and Conti-Ramsden (2008), suggest that although both phonological and broader language skills are important to literacy skill development in general, it is the broader language skills that are fundamental to comprehension.

The purpose for reading and the type of text under consideration are also important to comprehension. Recent research reviews (e.g., Gersten, Fuchs, Williams, & Baker, 2001; Vaughn, Gersten, & Chard, 2000) found that reading comprehension improved for children with learning disabilities (LD) and children at-risk when they learned how to determine word meaning, use prior knowledge, use cognitive strategies, and differentiate text structures. Figure 7.1 provides an illustration of some of the factors and interactions involved in comprehension. In general, the major types of text structures include narrative texts such as stories, and expository texts such as textbooks. Narrative texts usually include characters, a setting, and a plot with a sequence of events, a problem and solution. On the other hand, expository texts are informational in nature, and in general the purpose for reading is to obtain information in a content area.

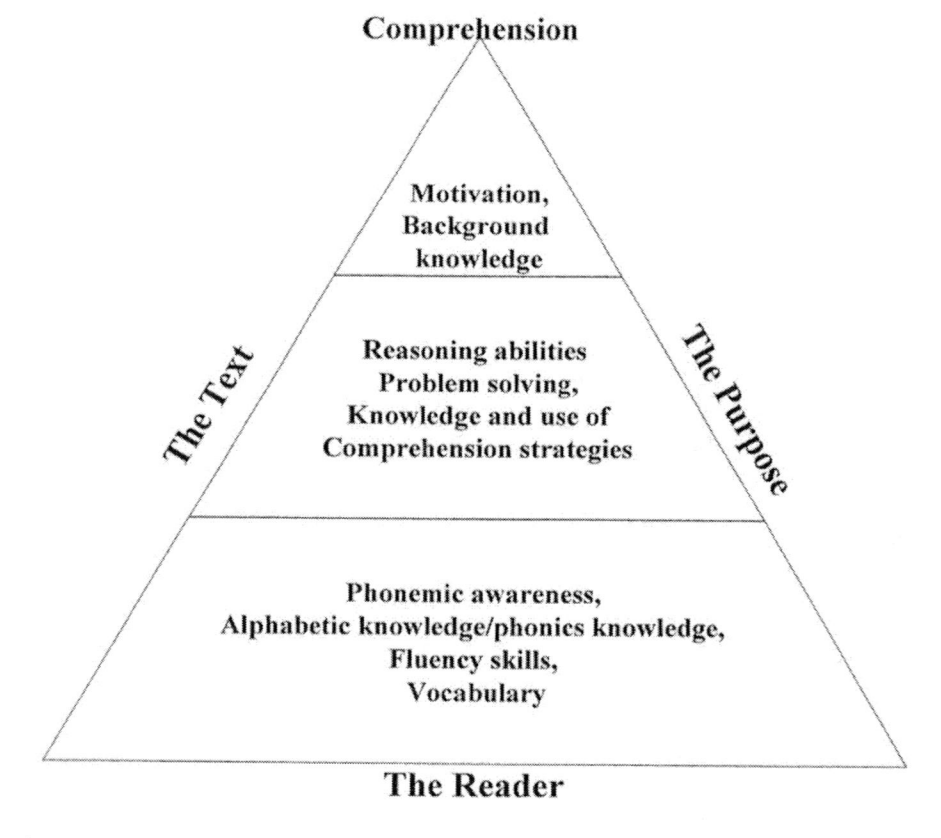

Figure 7.1. Comprehension: Foundations and Interations.

STRATEGY INSTRUCTION

Reading comprehension instruction should include a targeted focus on cognitive strategy instruction that includes strategies such as self-questioning, self-monitoring, and self-regulating. Cognitive strategies in reading include how an individual thinks about and acts during the processes of planning, carrying out, and evaluating reading performance. There has been extensive research in the area of cognitive strategy instruction that supports the use of explicit instruction to teach skills such as summarizing, asking and answering questions during reading, and self-monitoring of comprehension in order to improve reading comprehension (e.g., Gersten et al., 2001; Vaughn, Gersten, & Chard, 2000; National Reading Panel, 2000). When readers are taught to use these strategies efficiently and in combination, reading comprehension skills improve (Spafford, & Grosser, 2005).

One such strategy is called a think-aloud. In this strategy the teacher models a strategy by talking through the thought processes, thereby making an implicit strategy observable to children. Think-alouds help children see how the model makes predictions, links information to prior knowledge, monitors comprehension, and fixes problems with comprehension during reading. After the teacher models a strategy, children can then practice using the strategy with a partner.

Many strategies to promote reading comprehension can be divided temporally into pre-reading strategies, during reading strategies, and post-reading strategies. Pre-reading strategies to help children with comprehension of materials include the following: setting a purpose for reading; building background knowledge; linking background knowledge with text elements; encouraging predictions; and vocabulary review of words essential to understanding the selection. For example, children can be taught to use self-questioning strategies to access relevant domain or prior knowledge before reading to improve their comprehension (Vaughn, Gersten, & Chard, 2000). During reading comprehension strategies may include: asking questions while reading in order to monitor comprehension; and identifying specific problems and solutions. Post-reading comprehension strategies may include: generating questions about the text for others; linking background information to what was in the text; comparing predictions to actual text information; summarizing the story or text; creating a graphic organizer; and writing a reaction or opinion about the selection. In fact, the report of the NRP (2000) suggests that the following reading comprehension instructional strategies may be most effective when combined: comprehension monitoring; cooperative learning groups; question answering; question creation; and summarizing. Similarly, Keene and Zimmerman (1997) suggest that teachers and parents will foster the development of comprehension abilities when they help children to do the following: activate necessary prior knowledge and schema; utilize dual coding (create visual and sensory images); make inferences; ask questions; synthesize (summarize) selections; determine main ideas and themes; and address comprehension problems (fix-up/repair strategies).

Another comprehension building activity is providing children with opportunities to respond to texts. Children should be encouraged to respond not only orally in discussions and in writing in response journals or papers, but also in the arts through creative movement, music, poetry (chants, rhythms), drawing, and painting.

Vocabulary that is essential to understanding a selection should be identified and addressed instructionally. When a word is essential to understanding a text selection, it is necessary to determine whether the word is part of a child's listening vocabulary and whether or not context clues are sufficient to help figure out the word. Instructional scaffolding or support should be provided when either of these is lacking.

Comprehension monitoring is a metacognitive process that requires children to be aware of their own understanding as they read. Children can be taught to monitor how well they understand what they are reading. Part of the process of teaching a strategy is to teach children both how and when to use the strategy. When children develop metacognitive abilities, sometimes called metacomprehension, they are able to determine whether or not the text makes sense. Question generating approaches that encourage reader reflection enable readers to monitor their own comprehension (Spafford & Grosser, 2005). Teachers, parents, and even peers can provide a model of this process by talking through (verbalizing) their own thought processes as they read a passage aloud. This provides an example of just how an expert reader monitors his or her own comprehension, and how the generation of questions and answers, as well as summarizing, can help the reader clarify and more deeply understand a piece of writing. After children have a model of comprehension monitoring, they should have many opportunities to read interesting material with subsequent opportunities to discuss and practice comprehension strategies. Furthermore, it is important to remember that reading comprehension instruction should take place within the context of reading for real purposes. In addition, the focus of comprehension instruction changes from literal comprehension in the very early stages to inferential comprehension as children advance. Literal comprehension requires the child to remember or go back in the text to find answers that are explicitly stated within the text. On the other hand, answers to inferential questions require the child infer an answer which is not directly stated. The child must use context clues, background information and experiences, and reasoning abilities to come up with the answer to an inferential comprehension question. Inferential comprehension is a more complex type of comprehension and proves to be more difficult for many children. In addition, teachers and parents must be sensitive to the fact that the ability to infer requires practice just like any other skill.

As children begin to develop comprehension skills, it is also important to recognize that comprehension is not as simple as right and wrong answers to reading content questions. More specifically, comprehension is an interpretive process that develops out of the child's unique background, culture, and experiences, and different readers may comprehend the same selection in different ways (Rasinski, Padak, & Fawcett, 2010).

Similar to fluency instruction, multiple readings of a narrative selection can be used to reinforce inferential comprehension instruction. The first reading of the selection may include a teacher think-aloud so that the children have a model to emulate, while subsequent readings have students answer questions and explain their thinking and reasoning in how they arrived at their answers. Multiple readings may also be used with expository texts. Rereading a selection in order to focus on specialized vocabulary gives repeated exposure to new vocabulary words, as well as a closer examination of content, and may prove to be a helpful comprehension building strategy.

Children should engage in purposeful reading. In other words, the purpose for any reading activity should be established prior to reading. The purpose may be set by the teacher or by the child and helps focus on the important objectives of the reading session (e.g., enjoyment, fluency practice, or use of a comprehension strategy). Setting a purpose for reading helps children differentiate between information in the text that is relevant (worth remembering) and irrelevant (forgettable). Teachers may model purpose-setting through a think-aloud so that children observe how this is done and are able use this model to set their own purposes later. Reading comprehension is supported by purposeful reading.

A related factor is the importance that the reader attributes to the reading. For example, when reading for pleasure, the lack of understanding of a particular sentence or section may not initiate the use of a fix-up or repair strategy, while a lack of understanding in a sentence or section of a textbook chapter that is included in an upcoming exam may motivate the reader to employ a fix-up or repair strategy.

The goal of all reading instruction is to help children develop the skills that will support comprehension, because after all, the true essence of reading is comprehension. An important point to keep in mind is that time devoted to practice, similar to practice in anything else, will result in an improvement of skills. Reading comprehension is no exception. Systematic progress monitoring of reading comprehension is vital and goes hand-in-hand with increased time spent in real reading activities. Everything from observations and reading discussions to formal reading comprehension assessments will shed light on how children are progressing with specific skills. The information gathered should therefore be a guide for future instruction. Comprehension instruction should be a cumulative process, such that children build a foundation of skills and strategies that they will be able to use independently over time.

COMPREHENSION INSTRUCTION

A recommended sequence for reading comprehension instruction includes the following: daily review of previously learned material, followed by a teacher statement of the purpose of the upcoming lesson; presentation of the new instruction (new material to be learned); demonstration (model) using a think-aloud; guided practice, corrective feedback, and independent practice; a formative evaluation of student progress; and finally generalization practice (Faggella-Luby, & Deshler, 2008). Figure 7.2 provides an illustration of the teaching/learning cycle.

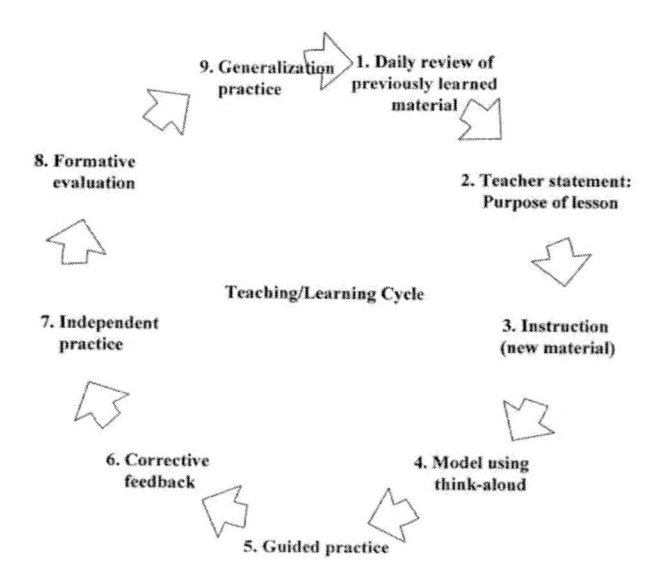

Figure 7.2. The Teaching/Learning Cycle.

Finally, the instructional arrangement, as well as specific actions during the teaching learning cycle, can have an impact on student learning. Research suggests that small group instruction and teacher prompting to use comprehension strategies are instructional components that help improve reading comprehension (Swanson, 1999).

Comprehension ideas for the Classroom

1) Retell/Free description: Individual children summarize and describe what they read.

   a) Prior to reading a passage, the teacher specifies the purpose for reading.
   b) Teacher models reading a passage and retelling the story details (1 min.).
   c) Teacher and student together discuss correct and incorrect responses.
   d) Student reads a passage.
   e) Student retells the story details (1 min.).
   f) Teacher notes correct and incorrect details and provides feedback.
   g) Student performance may be charted as a way to monitor progress.

2) Graphic Organizers: Helps students remember information in an organized visual manner. Key terms or concepts are presented visually and denote sequence and organization of the material, and relationships are displayed (event order, cause and effect).

   a) Story Map: Students map story elements in a visual manner.

      - Prior to reading a passage, the teacher specifies the purpose for reading.
      - Teacher presents information about a story grammar and the story elements that are included (characters, setting, problem, actions/events, and solution).
      - Students read the story.

- Teacher and students collaborate to come up with specific story elements.
- Students map the story elements on paper.
- Students orally retell story using the story map as a guide.
- Variation: Have students put an unorganized pile of story elements in the correct sequence.
- Teacher provides correction and feedback.

b) Anticipation Guides: Preview text concepts prior to reading:

- Students respond to statements prior to reading
- Students respond to statements after reading and compare with earlier answers

c) Descriptive graphic organizers: Illustrates attributes or features of the topic.
d) Sequential graphic organizers: Illustrates the time-order of events.
e) Compare and contrast graphic organizers: Venn Diagram to illustrate differences and similarities between concepts.
f) Cause and effect graphic organizer: Illustrates relationships between events and their consequences.
g) Problem solving graphic organizer: Illustrates problem elements and links to possible solutions.

3) Reciprocal Teaching: Small group discussion is used to facilitate reading comprehension. Teacher and students alternate roles as leader and responders (Palincsar & Brown, 1986).

a) Teacher specifies the purpose of instruction.
b) Teacher models using a think-aloud as the reading proceeds.

- Asking questions
- Summarizing information
- Clarifying questions
- Making predictions

c) Students read a story.
d) Students meet in small groups and teacher encourages students to take on the role of leader. Teacher provides as much scaffolding as necessary, until students are able to fully assume the role. (In addition to teacher support, cue cards may be provided at first).

- Students ask questions, clarify information for their peers, and make predictions.
- Students discuss the story.

4) Repeated Reading: Once the student reads a passage fluently, they work on comprehension.

a) Teacher specifies the purpose of the reading.
b) Teacher models a repeated reading.
c) Student reads a passage orally (collect and record one-minute sample)—student completes passage.
d) Add 10 to 15% to the rate as a target rate for next reading.
e) Student rereads the same passage (collect and record one-minute sample and compare with target).
f) This process may continue for several more readings if necessary
g) Teacher asks student to retell/summarize the story after final reading.
h) Teacher gives feed back.
i) Progress is monitored.

5) Guided Question Generation: Students work on one or two teacher selected questions at a time for each selection. Cards may be used to cue the questions.

a) Before reading:

- What is my purpose for reading?
- How will I "figure out" words/meanings I don't know?
- What do I already know?
- What do I think I will learn?
- What are my predictions about the text?

b) During reading:

- Am I reading fluently?
- Does the story/passage make sense?
- Am I using my "figure out" strategy?
- What is the passage all about?

c) After reading:

- What did I learn?
- Do I understand what I read? Do I need to go back and reread?
- Did I use my "figure out" strategy?
- Can I retell/summarize what happened?
- What was my purpose for reading? Did I accomplish it?

CHAPTER DISCUSSION QUESTIONS

1) Think about your own reading comprehension strategies. Imagine you are reading something, such as a textbook, and you don't comprehend a section. What do you do? Why?

2) What does the phrase "establish a purpose for reading" mean? How can you help students with learning disabilities understand what it means to establish a purpose?

CHAPTER APPLICATION EXERCISES

1) Select four examples of children's books that you believe you could use in your current or future classroom. Include both narrative and expository examples that are suitable for children in grades one through three. Prepare a lesson plan outline. Please indicate how you plan to activate or build students' background knowledge prior to reading or listening to the selections.

2) Plan and create a graphic organizer that will help children understand relationships in a science textbook (specific content). Be sure to

brainstorm with others which kind of graphic organizer will best fit with this purpose.

3) Select an award winning children's book. Parse the book into its story elements: characters, setting, problem, events, etc. Make a poster-size story map to share and discuss with others.

Chapter 8

ASSESSMENT AND INSTRUCTIONAL PLANNING

"Without a doubt, teaching reading and language is a job for a quick-
minded, informed, committed, flexible, and knowledgeable professional."
(Louisa Cook Moats, 2010, p.16)

ASSESSMENT

Assessment is defined here as the process of gathering information in order to make an informed education-related judgment or evaluation. There are many reasons for assessment in education. For example, assessments may be conducted in order to screen learners for potential problems, monitor progress during instructional cycles, determine eligibility and make a diagnosis for an individual child, or to plan instruction. Specifically with regard to literacy development, in order to plan and implement appropriate instruction, a thorough assessment of children's reading and writing skills is critical. Assessment and evaluation may be viewed as part of a continual and fluid process. Assessment is the gathering of information to make informed decisions about a child's future literacy instruction. It is a snapshot in time of how a child is doing in terms of particular skills such as phonemic awareness, alphabetic knowledge and phonics, word recognition, fluency, and comprehension. The result of the assessment is evaluation, or the actual judgment that is made regarding the information gathered—an interpretation of the information gathered. A comprehensive assessment includes informal and formal measures, observations of children's behavior, collection of products (such as writing samples), personal interviews with the child, information from the family, and reflections of the teachers who work with the child.

In addition, using assessment data will help document whether or not specific instructional practices are working at the school level and beyond, as well as at the individual level. The need for evidence-based practice, with continual documentation of progress is essential to determine what instructional methods work for which children. Assessment practices can be powerful in helping lower the number of children who struggle with literacy development. When teachers and schools do not provide adequate literacy instruction to children exhibiting signs of being at-risk of reading difficulty, the result is poor reading achievement (Justice, 2006). There is no excuse for lack of foresight in terms of prevention, and assessment is key.

The assessment and evaluation processes are based on goals and objectives that can be operationalized (observed in some way) and then measured. Once goals and objectives are determined, appropriate assessment instruments are selected to gather the information. The information is then analyzed and an evaluation is made as to what the next course of action will be in terms of appropriate instruction for the child. Instructional assessment, evaluation, informed instructional planning, and implementation of instruction are integral parts of the teaching/learning cycle. Throughout this process, it is also important to focus on the child's strengths—those abilities and qualities that are the foundation of success. The strengths may not be in what would typically thought of as school abilities but nevertheless may be those personal qualities that when nurtured lead to ultimate success. Some of these characteristics are often attributed to personality traits such as persistence and resilience. When teachers and parents find and nurture a child's strengths, whether they are in athletics, music, art or any other area, the child is more likely to develop self-confidence, self-esteem, and even motivation to try in other areas.

There are a few related concepts that are important to note. In broad terms assessment can be either formative or summative in nature. Formative assessment is used to help teachers make decisions during the process of learning to inform ongoing instruction, (e.g., weekly opportunity to respond), while summative assessment is used to evaluate instruction after the instructional time period is over or to sum up progress (e.g., a final examination). One way to look at the difference between these two forms of assessment is to see that summative assessment is more concerned with the product and formative assessment is more concerned with the process. They are both extremely useful. However their purposes are a bit different.

Both formal and informal assessments are used to examine literacy skills. Formal assessments are standardized instruments that have been normed and are reliable and valid. This means that the tests have been given to a large representative population sample and the results have been averaged. This allows for the comparison of scores between a group of children and the norm group or a child's scores and the norm group's performance on the literacy measures. Standard scores are used to make these comparisons. The term reliability refers to the consistency or stability of an individual's test scores, and the term validity refers to how well a test measures what it is supposed to measure. State and national regulations require such standardized tests. For example, legislation such as No Child Left Behind (NCLB) requires annual testing as part of state accountability requirements. This provides valuable information regarding how children are performing with respect to national standards, state standards, and even district standards.

Although formal standardized assessments provide important information, this chapter will focus on the informal assessment devices that teachers most commonly use in their daily instructional lives. Informal assessments are helpful in informing instruction. After all, the role of assessment in the teaching/learning process is to gather information in order to make judgments about instruction. Many assessment instruments are used that gather data in terms of numbers (the percentage of comprehension questions answered correctly, the words read correctly per minute, the number of words spelled correctly, etc.). Informal assessments include measures such as curriculum-based assessment (CBA), criterion-referenced (rubrics and checklists) assessments, and work product assessment such as portfolio assessment. Examples include surveys, checklists, miscue analyses, inventories, conferences, interviews, retellings, dialogue and response journals and portfolio assessments, etc. In addition to evaluating the data collected, teachers must evaluate the actual measures considered for assessing reading skills. That is, they must make judgments about the worth or value of a measure. Is the instrument reliable? Is the instrument valid?

Four basic types of assessments—each with a different purpose—are commonly used in schools. The basic types of assessments are illustrated in figure 8.1. First, screening assessments are quick to administer, conducted at the beginning of the year, and are provided for all students. Screening assessments help determine the instructional level of individual children and help determine the number of children functioning at, below, or above performance standards. The second basic type of assessment is progress-monitoring. These assessments are given to children during the year to determine whether children are learning (reaching the instructional objectives), and to assess critical skills for a grade level. The third basic type of assessment is diagnostic. These assessments are in-depth, for specific children who are struggling, or when screening assessment indicates need for more complete information. They are conducted when there is a need for more information than the screening assessment provided. The fourth basic type of assessment is the standardized outcome assessment and is administered to all children, typically every year. They are formal and are conducted to meet accountability standards.

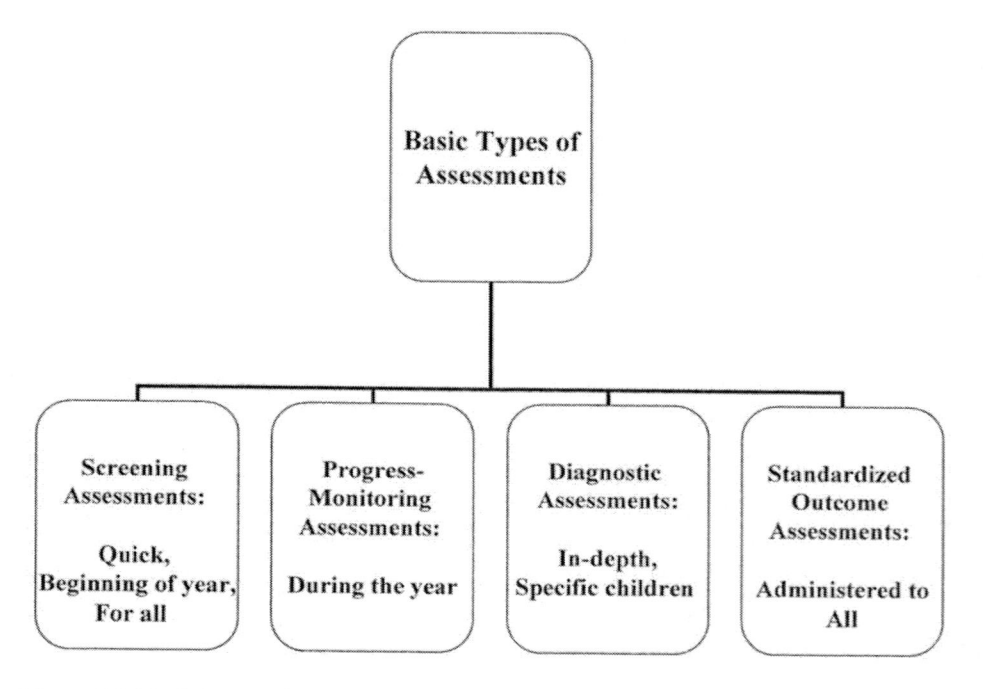

Figure 8.1. Basic Types of Assessments.

At the beginning of the year screening assessments should be used, and throughout the school year teachers should continuously use literacy assessment in order to monitor progress and make instructional changes when needed. Two examples of assessments that are commercially available and provide both a screening assessment and progress-monitoring assessment are AIMSWEB and DIBELS.

There are many advantages to informal assessments. First, the results of informal assessments can be directly applied to the instructional program and assessment is integrated with instruction so that the time away from teaching/learning is minimized. Furthermore, informal assessments can be administered easily, quickly, as frequently as needed, and they are inexpensive. Informal assessments also have limitations. A specific instrument may be limited in scope and not suitable for a specific need, and the time and required to develop an instrument may be prohibitive. There is also the issue of subjectivity in selection of an instrument. That is, a teacher may choose to use one instrument over another one due to personal preference.

The following is a possible sequence in the assessment process to inform instruction for students who are struggling with literacy skills (see figure 8.2):

- Identify general difficulties observed through survey instruments.
- Confirm problem areas with diagnostic tests.
- Select informal assessment instruments to probe specific aspects of the skills in question.
- Design lessons that enable the further collection of data within the teaching/learning cycle (continuous progress monitoring).
- Use the results of the progress monitoring to modify instruction.
- Continue with progress monitoring.

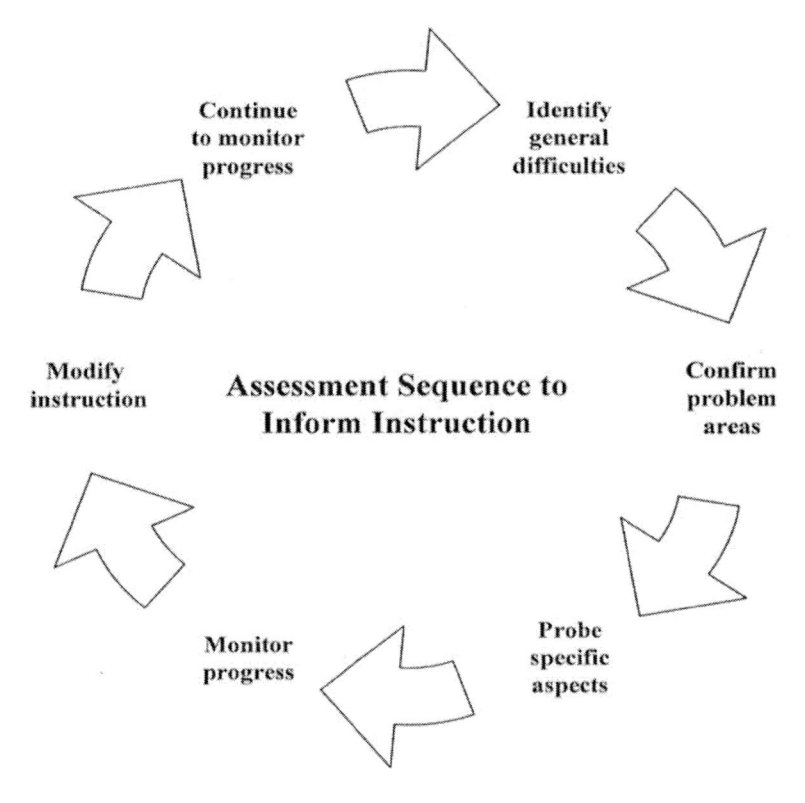

Figure 8.2. Assessment Sequence to Inform Instruction.

Two vital aspects of literacy instructional decision making are placement within a literacy program (level) and the selection of appropriate reading materials to suit different purposes. An informal reading inventory (IRI) is an example of an assessment that teachers can use to determine a child's independent reading level, instructional reading level, frustration level, and listening capacity. An informal reading inventory usually includes a series of graded reading passages along with graded word lists. These can be used to determine reading competence levels, and to highlight specific skill deficiencies and strengths. Four reading levels are commonly derived and include: The independent level, which is characterized by fluent reading, high accuracy, and high recall and comprehension; the instructional level which presents some difficulty but children can profit from instruction and support; the frustration level which is characterized by a notable breakdown in fluency and accuracy, and comprehension suffers; and the capacity level or listening comprehension which is a measure of listening comprehension and is sometimes used to determine an expected comprehension level. Although percentages for the levels vary a bit from one authority to another, this author uses the following percentages to determine levels for selecting materials for students: Independent level—the child has 98% or above word recognition and 90% comprehension; Instructional level—95% word recognition and 75 percent comprehension; Frustration level—less than 90% word recognition, and 50% comprehension.

This means that when the teacher or parent wants to provide children with opportunities to read on their own (independent level) the material should be easy enough that the child recognizes 98 out of 100 words in a selection. This allows the child to practice reading with relative ease and helps to give the child a sense of success and independence. The child can focus on areas of reading such as fluency and comprehension, rather than on decoding words.

The instructional level is the level at which instruction should be geared. The child should still need help and support (scaffolding) in order to reach their highest potential with their newly developing literacy skills, yet the material is not so difficult that the child is disheartened or wants to give up due to frustration. At this level the child may need instruction for approximately 5 words out of 100 in a selection, and he or she may need comprehension instruction to aid their understanding of connected text.

When a child has trouble with approximately 10 words out of 100 or has 50% or less comprehension, the material is too difficult and is likely to cause frustration. This level should be avoided since it may cause the child to dislike reading, have low self-efficacy for his/her reading skills, and avoid reading tasks.

An IRI will also help identify a child's strengths and weaknesses in word recognition, fluency, and comprehension. There are several commercially available Informal Reading Inventories (e.g., *Bader Reading and Language Inventory, 2009; Burns and Roe Informal Reading Inventory, 2007*). An IRI usually includes word lists and passages. Children may be assessed with oral and silent reading, as well as listening comprehension. The passages are often used to obtain fluency information, as well as comprehension information. A miscue analysis (looking at error patterns) can be used to indicate problem areas in word recognition skills.

In addition to published informal reading inventories, teachers can gain valuable information from using their own informal reading inventory procedure. In the informal reading inventory procedure, graded passages of connected text of approximately 100 words each are selected. Beginning with the child's estimated independent level, the child reads several graded passages orally, and the teacher records accuracy rate (percentage of words read correctly), reading rates (words read correctly per minute), and asks comprehension questions. If the child struggles with the first passage given (makes more than five errors per 100 words, an easier passage should be presented. Just like a published informal reading inventory, using this procedure, the teacher can determine the independent, instructional, and frustration reading levels for the child. In addition, a miscue analysis can be used to examine the types of errors the child makes. Using this practical method, teachers can gain important information about the child's reading level, types of errors in word recognition, fluency, and comprehension.

INSTRUCTIONAL PLANNING

What is learning? What is teaching? What different types of learning take place in schools? Behaviorists discuss learning in terms of changes in behavior due to experience with a focus on relationships among observable stimuli and responses. On the other hand, cognitivists discuss learning in terms of changes in mental associations due to experience with a focus on the role of the internal mental processes in learning. When trying to gain a perspective on how theories can inform education, it is important to note that theories help to explain and predict the conditions under which learning is most likely to occur. However, no single theory can be considered fact.

Think back to your days in school. What did you learn? One of the themes of education is reflective practice or reflection in action. Reflection in action incorporates self-reflection, analysis, and evaluation in the teaching-learning cycle. Teachers should always ask these questions: How do I size up this learning environment?; and Is this truly a learning community? In thinking about creating a learning community, other questions deserve consideration.

- What role does the teacher play?
- What role does the curriculum play?
- What role do the children play?

Effective practices in education are those designed to, and do in fact, achieve optimal results for all children. However, it is important to remember that children are individuals—each with his or her own unique characteristics, abilities, and talents, and there is no one method that works for all children. Effective teachers possess many qualities including the ability to create a learning environment that values all learners. For example, effective teachers have cultural sensitivity, high expectations, are attentive to developmental appropriateness, have an understanding of children with special needs, know how to access educational resources to help solve problems, and use technology appropriately. Therefore, teachers must be problem solvers, knowledgeable about content, knowledgeable about child development, effective communicators, goal oriented, and well-organized. Teaching is a complex process with great responsibilities. Think of the number of decisions that a teacher makes in a single day, a week, a semester, a school year. The number is staggering, and the ramifications may last a lifetime. A teacher wears many hats during the day.

Lesson planning is vital to effective teaching. A lesson plan is an organizational tool that links assessment and instruction and provides teachers with a way to evaluate whether or not instructional goals are being met. A lesson plan is a guide that gives instruction a format or structure. In a sense, a lesson plan is a map that gives direction to the teaching-learning cycle. A lesson plan organizes learning events (teaching and learning activities) in order to reach specific educational objectives. For beginning teachers in particular, quality lesson planning can add to an increase in a teacher's self-efficacy in instruction. That is, a well-designed lesson plan may help with confidence in teaching.

Lesson plans provide a structure that allows others to "peek in" to a teacher's thinking about instruction. Students in college teacher preparation programs develop very detailed lesson plans as they learn about the teaching-learning cycle and develop their teaching skills. School principals often require that teachers submit their weekly lesson plans—usually in a much less detailed format.

Lesson planning includes identification of the needs of the children that will be the focus of the lesson; identification of the instructional goals, specific learning objectives, state standards, prior knowledge needed, concepts, and content; determination of teaching methods (type of instruction, instructional grouping, etc.); materials, procedures, and reinforcement activities; and assessment and evaluation. In addition, lesson planning should include reflection on the strengths and weaknesses of lessons. What worked and for whom? What can be changed to enhance learning for all children? Lesson plans should be based on educational goals and guided by research-based theory. In addition, they should be informed by assessment results, and should promote student engagement in appropriate learning experiences across the three domains of learning (cognitive, affective, psycho-motor).

Although there are different formats for lesson plans (narrative, bulleted, step-by-step, graphic), most lesson plan requirements include the following: designation of demographics; specification of subject area of instruction; statement of need for instruction; description of instruction; list of supporting materials and resources; specification of methods of assessment of student learning; and evaluation of teaching (reflection). The goals and objectives are the driving force behind a lesson plan. They set the stage. Children need to be made aware of what is to be learned, why it is important, how it relates to what they already know, and how it relates to their own lives in language that is easily understood by all children.

Gagne's events of instruction (Gagne & Driscoll, 1988) are based on information processing theory and help explain why certain lesson plan sequences and structures support learning. In Gagne's model there are nine events of instruction that are used to support the processes or three phases of learning. The first phase of learning is the preparation phase and includes the following events of instruction: gaining attention (promoting alertness); informing the learner of the objective (promoting expectancy); and stimulating recall of background or prior knowledge (activation of working memory). The next phase of learning is the acquisition and performance phase and is the heart of instruction. The fourth event of instruction is the presentation of the stimulus material (new material presentation) and may be in many different formats (modeling, demonstration, graphics, discussion, text, etc.). The next two events of instruction, providing learning guidance and eliciting performance, are very important. Providing learning guidance in a meaningful way supports the child's development of schema and long-term memory storage and retrieval. In order for children to move from skill acquisition to being able to perform the skill on their own they need ample opportunities to successfully practice new skills. In other words, when new information is meaningful and a child has ample opportunity to practice newly acquired skills (eliciting performance), they have a better chance of being able to retrieve the information from long-term memory. In addition, the seventh event of instruction, feedback, is important to the learning process. Both positive reinforcement and feedback to correct inaccuracies are used to support learning. The eighth and ninth events of instruction make up the transfer phase of learning. This has to do with how well children are able to generalize what they have learned. This means that information learned in one situation can be used in another situation or setting. Assessment is used to gauge whether or not children have reached the instructional objectives of the lesson. Assessment is done in a variety of ways in a variety of situations to determine how well children have generalized the learning. Using information in new ways and situations enhances retention and transfer with deeper processing, thereby making a more elaborate schema with more cues for information retrieval later.

Questioning and modeling how to generate questions are essential elements of instruction and should be incorporated in all lessons. There are two basic types of questions, and they are referred to as convergent and divergent. Convergent questions converge or are relatively narrow in scope and may be considered explicit with the answers stated directly in the text. On the other hand, divergent questions are more open-ended and require more critical thinking and may be considered implicit or inferential. That is, the answers are not directly stated in the text. Both questioning strategies are important to the learning process, and teachers need to be proficient users of both types. It is important to include both types of questions in lesson plans. In addition, instructional grouping should be a consideration when planning questions. Some children may not want to respond to questions in a whole group discussion, yet they may participate or answer the same questions in a smaller group. In addition, it is important to extend children's answers to questions. For example, when asking a divergent or open-ended question, if a child gives a vague or short response, use clarifying questioning techniques to extend or expand on a child's answer.

Another important technique to use when asking questions is to allow for sufficient time to pass before calling on a child. In other words, ask a question, pause to allow more children time to formulate an answer, and then call on someone to answer. This allows children enough processing time to think about and respond to a question. Another helpful technique is to encourage summarizing. Initially, the teacher may pause at intervals throughout a discussion or lesson to summarize the main points. Later, children may be asked to summarize or retell important points. This is a very helpful technique that promotes comprehension.

There are many layers to effective instructional planning. Teachers must be very knowledgeable of the content and pedagogy, and they must understand the unique characteristics of the students they teach. In addition, teachers must be able to take that underlying knowledge of content and child development and then design and sequence lessons that best meet children's needs. Finally, appropriate assessment strategies that are linked to the lesson plan objectives and goals must be utilized to measure whether or not children are making adequate progress.

Writing Lesson Plans

Initially a detailed lesson plan format is recommended in order to gain knowledge and expertise in lesson planning. After pre-service teachers master this format (i.e., it becomes second nature), and as beginning teachers go out and work in the field of education, other formats may be experimented with or developed for personal use. There are many acceptable formats. The following is a modified version of one commonly used at The College of Saint Rose, in Albany, New York.

Lesson Plan Format

- LESSON TITLE: The title encapsulates the heart of the lesson.
- DEMOGRAPHICS: Include: grade level/age range, setting (time and place), number of students, and any staffing considerations. Identify any learner characteristics that will be necessary to consider and accommodate in this lesson.
- LESSON PURPOSE: This section describes the purpose, states any prerequisite knowledge needed, states the lesson goals/objectives, and lists any individualized objectives for students with special needs.

  - ➢ Prerequisites: The prior learning that is necessary for pupils to have in order to experience success in the lesson.
  - ➢ Lesson Goals/Lesson Objectives: This section makes the substance of the lesson clear. The substance of the lesson may be communicated in a variety of forms (i.e., benchmarks, concepts, dispositions, generalizations, goals, objectives, outcomes, processes, or skills).
  - ➢ Individualized Objective(s): Individualized objectives (I.E.P. related) for learners with special needs.

RATIONALE:

- Content: The Rationale should explain the connection between the Statement(s) of Intent and the Procedures, and the Rationale answers the questions, "Why teach this content?" and "Why use the particular methodology you have chosen?"
- NYS Standards: Content rationale is drawn from New York State Learning Standards, New York State Curriculum Guides, national, regional, state, and local professional associations (e.g., NCTM, NCSS, NAST, NCTE), local curriculum guides and other sources that help teachers select curriculum.
- Methodology: A rationale for methodology is drawn from research-based findings (e.g., of how particular pupils learn best, educational psychology principles, learning theory that informs age-appropriate pedagogy).

PROCEDURES: This section details, in a step-by-step manner, the implementation of the lessons. It is clear from this section of the plan that:

- The teacher has thought through the lesson from start to finish.
- Procedures are aligned with both Statement(s) of Intent and Rationale.
- Techniques or strategies that will be used to assess the students' attainment of learning outcomes are included in the Procedures.
- The teacher candidate recognizes that when working with a diverse population, one needs a wide repertoire of models to meet a wide variety of needs.
- The teacher candidate has included required accommodations and/or modifications (such as those identified in a Section 504 Plan, an IEP, or for ESL pupils).

PROCEDURAL FORMAT

- Introduction: List the steps the teacher takes to introduce the lesson. Specify how you will engage pupils in subsequent instruction. For example, one may begin with a preset, an advance organizer, a signal for attention, a pivotal question, a discrepant set of facts, an invitation to activate prior knowledge, or a preview of a lesson.

- Body: List the steps the teacher takes to develop the lesson. Delineate the substance of content to be delivered or investigated. Identify methods the teacher will use; for example, one might specify techniques for facilitating pupil participation, questions and anticipated responses, transitions, or specific techniques for guiding and monitoring instruction.
- Assessment of Learning: List the steps the teacher takes to determine if the statement(s) of intent of the instruction are met. Note that assessment may be embedded as one or more procedural steps throughout or at the end of the lesson.
- Closure: List the step(s) the teacher takes to end the lesson. Steps the teacher takes to help pupils reach closure may involve, for example, asking a thought-provoking question, reviewing the major concepts of the lesson, articulating generalizations, or completing a K-W-L chart.
- Follow-up for generalization: List embedded or additional steps the teacher may take to assist pupils in maintaining and transferring the learning from this lesson and applying it to other situations.

TEACHER REFLECTION: In this section, the teacher evaluates the written plan and its implementation, and may discuss implications for future teaching and learning (possible modifications to the lesson).

RESOURCES

- Materials.
- Works Cited or References (of sources cited in lesson plan).
- Bibliography of Teacher Resources (additional sources that may be useful to the teacher).
- Bibliography of Pupil Resources (additional sources that may be useful to the pupils).

QUESTIONS FOR REFLECTION AND DISCUSSION

1) Discuss the uses and limitations of assessment instruments.
2) Explain how teachers can evaluate instruction and monitor progress of children with special needs.
3) Reflect on the idea of bias in testing. Discuss the possible ways assessment instruments or procedures may be biased and what can be done to remedy the situation.

CHAPTER APPLICATION EXERCISES

1) Interview a teacher to learn about their experiences with the referral, evaluation, and classification process of students with special needs. Find out how he/she uses informal assessments in the classroom, and how he/she plans for the instructional needs of all students.
2) Administer three reading passages from an Informal Reading Inventory to a child who has reading difficulties. Follow the procedures for administration. Record the fluency rate, the accuracy rate, and conduct a miscue analysis of the errors. Write a one page report of your findings.

Chapter 9

READING PROGRAM ESSENTIALS

"I read my eyes out and can't read half enough. ...The more one reads the
more one sees we have to read."
(John Adams, 1794)

CORE READING INSTRUCTION

Core reading instruction (a term that is commonly used in RTI) provides the basis for instruction in reading. Estimates suggest that high quality core reading instruction should enable approximately 80% of children to reach their reading goals (Hoover & Patton, 2008; Rasinski, Padak, & Fawcett, 2010). A core program should be used in conjunction with strategies and other materials to provide children with a comprehensive program of instruction. Supplemental programs and resources are used to support a core reading program, while an intervention program is used to support children who need more intensive instruction. Therefore, any core program that is adopted by a school system should be research-based and provide systematic instruction in phonemic awareness, phonics and word analysis, vocabulary, fluency, and comprehension. Furthermore, it is essential that a research-based program of instruction in reading be implemented as it was intended. That is, in order to get the most out of an instructional program and obtain the best results for children, it should be followed with fidelity. These elements are summarized in Figure 9.1. Instruction should be carried out with consistency, with clarity, explicitly, with scaffolding, and children should be provided with ample opportunities for successful practice applying new skills (first with support, then independently).

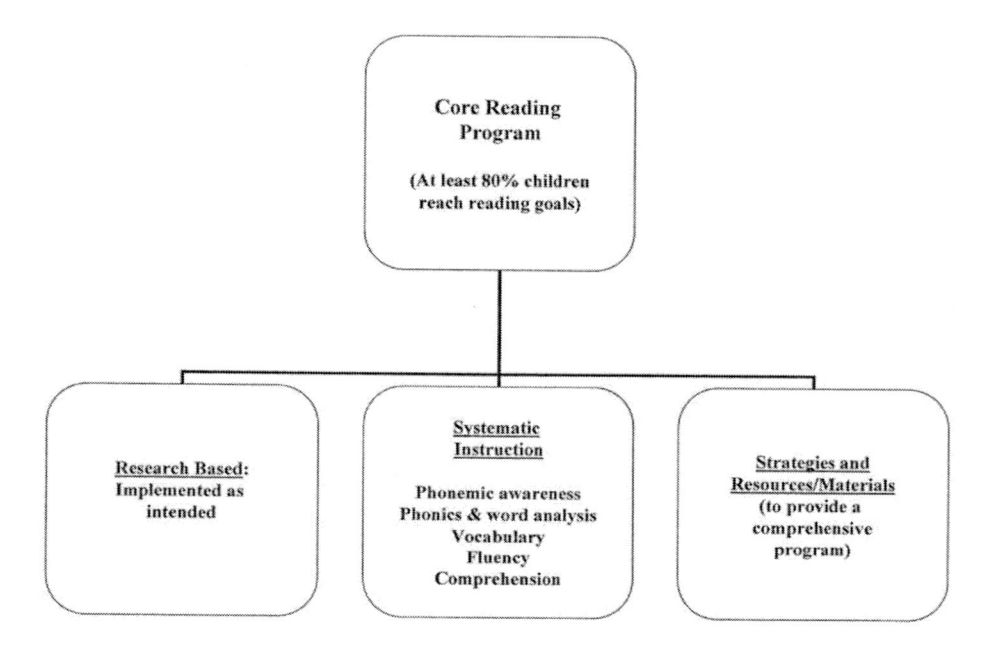

Figure 9.1. Core Reading Instruction Elements.

Another essential element in literacy instruction is the instructional time devoted to this critical area of education. The amount of time during the school day allocated for literacy instructional time must be a priority. A related essential consideration in implementing any reading program is instructional grouping. Instructional grouping refers to the size of the groups (whole class, small group, or individual), the organization (peer, cooperative, teacher directed), and the location of instruction.

Essential Skills

There are many essential skills that should be addressed in a core reading program and the progression should follow a path that leads children from the simple to the more complex as they master skills and move from one grade level to the next. Figure 9.2 presents phonemic awareness instructional targets and considerations.

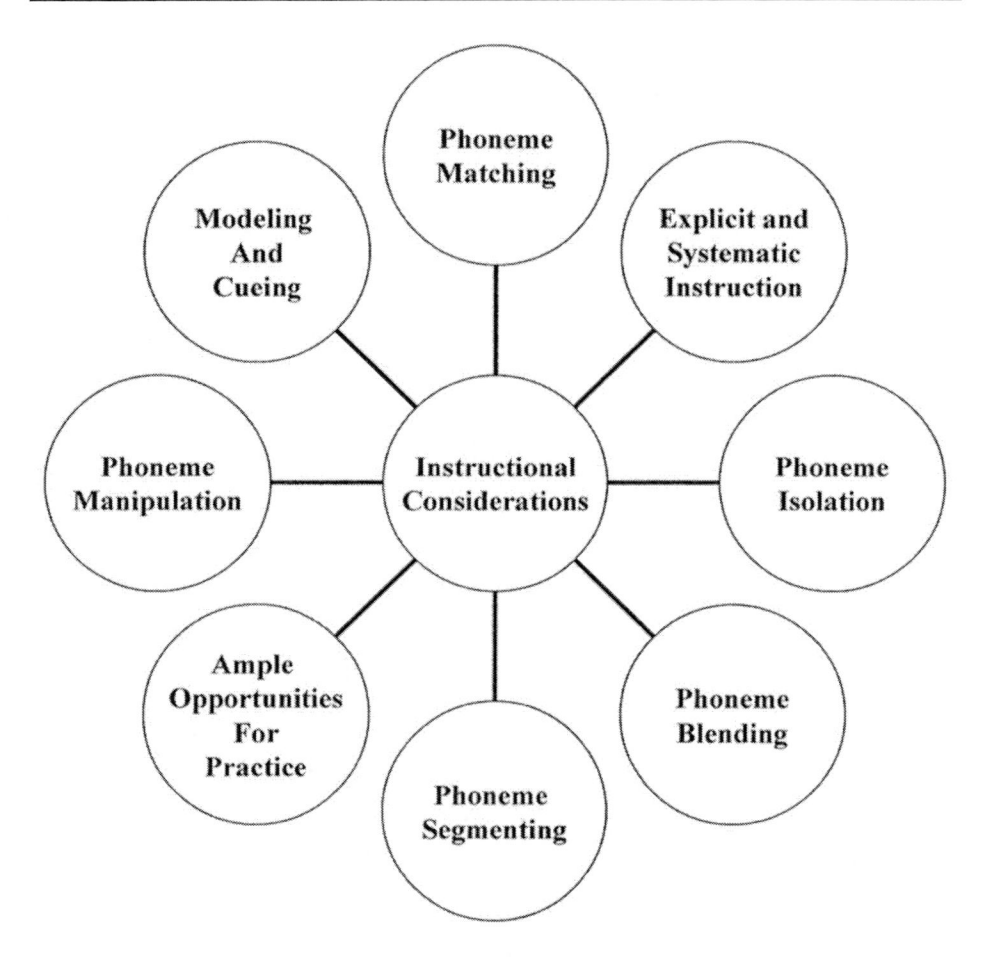

Figure 9.2. Phonemic Awareness: Instructional Considerations.

Although reference is made to grade levels, instruction should always be based on individual need and differentiated accordingly. The following instructional suggestions are geared toward children in the primary grades—kindergarten through third grade.

As children move through the primary grades, instruction should focus on those activities that help children become aware of the sounds of language and should emphasize the joy in playing with language. Instruction should progress from easier tasks such as isolating phonemes, to more difficult such as blending phonemes and segmenting phonemes in order that children remember the internal details of spoken words (Moats, 2010; Carnine, et al., 2010). Modeling and explicit instruction, with extensive opportunities for children to respond and practice, integration of letter-sound correspondence instruction to phonemic awareness, and the use of signals or cues to move from one sound to the next within words (manipulatives, hand movements, voiced signals) are all instructional practices that promote phonemic awareness skill development (National Reading Panel Report, 2000).

According to Moats (2010, p. 203), "The ability to decode words fluently using letter-sound correspondences is the cornerstone for early reading success." In kindergarten phonics skills should be introduced in a well-planned sequence beginning with the most useful letters first. Teachers should model each new letter-sound correspondence and children should practice them until they are able to automatically identify and produce the targeted phoneme/grapheme correspondences, since "accurate association of phonemes with graphemes permits and fosters a child's automatic recognition of whole words as reading fluency is acquired (Moats, 2010, p. 203). Regular review of previously learned phonics skills should be incorporated in the teaching and learning cycle. To avoid confusion, it is advisable to plan instruction so that children can easily differentiate between any letters or sounds that are introduced during a lesson (i.e., do not introduce the letters b and d on the same day). To foster the process of blending and segmenting real words, it is helpful to introduce and practice the most useful short vowels early in the instructional sequence. Similarly, it is beneficial to teach irregular sight words that are common in beginning level texts (e.g., *the, of, said, has*), but advisable to avoid the simultaneous introduction of words that look similar (e.g., *was, saw*). It is also important that children have many opportunities within lessons to practice blending (e.g., decodable word lists) and many opportunities to begin to use newly learned skills in real reading. A transitional period, between initial learning of the letter/sound correspondences and real reading (e.g., trade books), may include the use of decodable or controlled connected text. In order to assure that children learn skills to a mastery level, it is important to continually assess and monitor how they are doing. One way to encourage mastery learning and avoid confusion is to limit the amount of new information introduced at any one time.

Kindergarten is a wonderful time to develop and expand the vocabulary skills of young children and should include explicit instruction of new vocabulary and concepts. There are several things that should guide instruction. First, vocabulary words should be taught based on how useful they are for understanding an immediate text selection, as well as how useful they are for future understanding. Teachers should make sure that explanations are clear and are meaningful to children (i.e., linked to prior knowledge), and when children do not have the needed prior knowledge, teachers should try to provide the needed experiences through discussions, virtual field trips, hands-on activities, and exposure through oral language stories and read-alouds. These kinds of classroom experiences will help to build necessary background knowledge for future learning. In other words, children should be given the opportunity to experience critical vocabulary words many times in different contexts. In this way, children are supported toward the goal of deeper processing of vocabulary by linking prior knowledge of known words with new words. Other helpful techniques teachers can use to foster vocabulary development include modeling new words in sentences, asking children to talk about meanings in their own words, and providing consistent and continual review of vocabulary words.

Listening comprehension can be developed in kindergarten through various teaching strategies. For example, teachers may explicitly teach and model comprehension strategies through think-alouds. A think-aloud is a strategy in which teachers verbalize their internal thinking processes to explain how they arrived at an answer. Teachers may also identify and teach narrative and expository text structures by pointing out features during big book read-alouds. In addition, kindergarten teachers should identify and teach new vocabulary words that are critical to understanding a specific selection, and they can help children make connections to their prior knowledge to improve listening comprehension. Children should have many opportunities to listen to different types of texts with many opportunities to discuss the selections and practice comprehension strategies. During read-alouds, teachers should use questioning techniques at natural points in order to gauge comprehension and clarify any misconceptions. Finally, instruction should be planned, organized, and focused with the developmental ages of the children in mind.

In sum, children in the beginning of their literacy and school experiences need explicit and systematic instruction in phonemic awareness, phonics, vocabulary, and listening comprehension. See Table 9.1 for an overview of phonics, vocabulary, and listening skills for kindergarten. Instruction at this level should provide rich opportunities for children to practice newly acquired skills and review learned skills. Teachers should also extend and scaffold skill development and link fundamental skills to future skills.

The skills for the first grade continue to build toward literacy success and are similar to kindergarten skills, yet they extend and build on the previously learned skills. That is, there is a hierarchy—with much overlap, review and reinforcement—in building these foundational skills. At this point in their development children should receive plenty of practice blending, segmenting, and manipulating the sounds in oral language, as the letters of the alphabet are systematically and progressively linked to phonemic awareness activities. For example, the instructional sequence would begin with work on initial position phonemes, followed by final position phonemes, followed by medial position phonemes.

Table 9.1. Literacy Skills in Kindergarten

Literacy Skills in Kindergarten

Phonics Skills	Vocabulary Skills	Listening Skills
Use explicit instruction and modeling	Use explicit instruction for new vocabulary and concepts	Use think-alouds to model comprehension strategies
Introduce most useful letters first	Check prior knowledge & use *everyday* language in explanations	Identify important vocabulary, link to prior knowledge, and reinforce
Teach to automaticity	Link known words to new words	Teach story grammar and text structure elements
Present letters/sounds that are easily distinguished	Provide opportunities to experience vocabulary words many times & in different contexts	Provide many opportunities for listening to and discussing narrative and expository texts
Teach useful short vowels early	Review vocabulary words consistently	Ask questions strategically— before, during, and after
Provide many opportunities to practice decodable words in real reading of decodable text	Scaffold vocabulary development with many read-alouds	Provide many opportunities to practice comprehension strategies
Introduce (pre-teach) useful sight words (e.g., *the, said, of*)	Model vocabulary words in sentences/classroom interactions	Model and provide opportunities for story retellings

The instructional sequence should also be progressive in nature meaning that the focus moves from words with two and three phonemes to words with four phonemes, and so forth. Similarly, word recognition instruction should be systematic and progress from CVC words that begin with continuous sounds (e.g., *man*), to CVC words that begin with stop sounds (e.g., *cat*), to CCVC words that contain initial consonant blends (e.g., *stop*), to CVCC words that contain final consonant blends (e.g., *fast*). Teachers should model, use explicit instruction, and scaffold learning. When children are able to use previously learned letter/sound combinations to facilitate learning of new words, word learning becomes a building or construction process. To facilitate this process and help children increase their word recognition fluency, word family and word pattern instruction and activities are helpful instructional strategies. In first grade, decodable texts may also be used as a transition (between decoding words and authentic reading of texts) so that children have opportunities to successfully apply their newly acquired phonics skills in reading connected text. However, some useful irregular words are necessary to avoid texts that sound contrived and lack interest. Thus, teachers should introduce or pre-teach strategic irregular words that are needed prior to reading a particular selection and give children many opportunities to successfully practice and review their growing list of mastered sight words.

Fluency in reading connected text is an important skill that is related to vocabulary and comprehension. In first grade children should have many opportunities to practice, and have success, reading connected text as soon as they have mastered the required words in passages. That is, the passages contain words that children have learned to decode (include regular letter-sound correspondences that have been learned), along with any necessary previously learned irregular sight words. Then children are encouraged to practice reading passages with appropriate rate, emphasis, pausing, and expression. The passages chosen for fluency practice should be at the independent level, meaning that children should demonstrate an accuracy level of 98% or higher for the words included in the selection used for fluency practice.

First grade vocabulary instruction should include modeling, explicit instruction, and should link children's prior knowledge to new words and concepts. Learning is supported (i.e., scaffolded) and deeper processing is encouraged, when relationships between words and connections between known words and new words are made clear. Vocabulary words are selected for instruction when they are critical to comprehension and future learning. To reinforce vocabulary learning, children need many opportunities (and in different contexts) to experience new words and meanings. Instruction in vocabulary should be systematic with regular review of previously learned words. Moreover, vocabulary development should be supported and extended through interactive oral language experiences with stories, poems, songs, and expository texts.

Reading comprehension instruction in first grade should include explicit instruction in comprehension strategies such as self-questioning, and comprehension monitoring. In addition, reading comprehension instruction should include teacher modeling or think-alouds to show children how to find the main idea, find supporting details (literal comprehension), retell or summarize a story, make predictions, and answer inferential questions. In order to reduce memory load and increase attention and focus on comprehension, shorter passages may be used at first. Teachers should activate children's prior knowledge or help them make connections between what they already know and the new information presented, and instruction should provide many opportunities for guided practice in using comprehension strategies, as well as include systematic review of strategies previously learned. In addition, children need instruction regarding expository and narrative texts in order to recognize different text structures and components. They should have ample opportunities to listen to, read, and discuss various types of texts and the progression should flow logically from easier text structures to more complex structures. That is, instruction should begin with simple story grammars that have readily identifiable elements to more complex stories (i.e., those with subplots, etc.).

As they move through school, children in the primary grades are building on their phonemic awareness skills in new letter-sound correspondences and word recognition activities. In addition, they are learning to recognize patterns that help with automaticity and reading fluency. At this point children need many opportunities for successful practice with these newly acquired critical skills and explicit and systematic instruction in new skill development. They also need regular cumulative review of previously learned skills so that they have the building blocks to progress to higher level literacy skills.

In second grade, phonics and word analysis instruction is ongoing. The acquisition of new skills should begin with explicit instruction (e.g., prefixes, suffixes, word parts, word patterns). Then word analysis skills can be supported and practiced within real reading experiences with narrative and expository texts. In addition, teachers should teach word analysis strategies for reading multisyllabic words and model how to use the strategies. After strategies are taught (e.g., using word parts and patterns to figure out unknown words), children need plenty of opportunities to successfully practice the newly acquired skills in order to master the skills and increase their word recognition fluency. Practice in using new word analysis skills should also be encouraged when children have the chance to read a wide variety of materials so they generalize their new skills across settings. Similarly, children need to be supported in making connections between their decoding skills in reading and their spelling skills in written expression.

Irregular words that children will encounter frequently should be taught explicitly before they experience them in print. Teachers should provide activities that allow for successful practice and regular cumulative review of common irregular words. To promote proficient reading, these words should be learned to the point of mastery or automaticity. That is, they become sight words. It is important to plan instruction so that the number of essential words presented is not so many that children's memory capacity is taxed.

Reading fluency is promoted for second grade learners when they have ample practice with a wide variety of reading materials at their independent level (i.e., 98% or above accuracy) and they are encouraged to read smoothly, with attention to punctuation, and the meaning of the selection. Instruction may include fluency strategies such as repeated reading, pair-share reading, choral reading, and readers' theatre. In all of these strategies the intent is to provide children with successful practice in the oral reading of a variety of connected text selections so that they become more fluent readers and gain confidence in themselves as readers.

Vocabulary instruction in second grade follows the progression begun in the years prior. This means that specific essential words and concepts are taught explicitly; meanings are related in children's everyday language in order to make connections between prior knowledge and new knowledge; words and concepts are selected based on usefulness; and children are given many opportunities for successful review of vocabulary words and concepts. An essential element in working toward successful vocabulary building is that children are supported in making connections between new words and known words. Instruction in synonyms and antonyms and advanced word analysis, skills such as using word parts to predict meaning, support vocabulary development. Additionally, children are supported in processing meanings through multiple and varied exposures (deeper level processing) to words over time and in using context (comprehension strategy) to determine meaning. Strategies may be taught explicitly through think-alouds. Children should be given many opportunities to extend their vocabulary through listening, speaking, reading, and writing.

Reading comprehension instruction builds on previous skills and comprehension strategies such as summarization and comprehension monitoring and teachers should build and extend these skills through modeling and teacher-guided practice. As children progress through school, text structure complexity increases. Therefore, text structures such as story grammars in narrative texts, and chapter headings, subheadings, graphs, and charts in informational texts need to be part of a carefully planned and organized system of comprehension instruction. Reading comprehension is enhanced when the following occurs: any required prior knowledge is determined and then activated; children are provided with many opportunities for successful practice; strategies are reviewed in a variety of different texts; and organizational tools such as graphic organizers are modeled and practiced to stimulate comparing, contrasting, organizing, and visually illustrating ideas and concepts.

Children at this stage need explicit and systematic instruction to foster continued skill development. In addition, children need a systematic and cumulative review of phonics skills, vocabulary skills, fluency, and reading comprehension strategies to support higher level skill development as they progress through the grade levels. They also need many opportunities for successful practice of their newly acquired skills and strategies in real reading of connected texts at their independent level.

In third grade, children continue to build on their previously mastered phonics and word analysis skills. Assessment should be on-going and any gaps in knowledge should be addressed. In so doing, children need explicit instruction in advanced word analysis for decoding multi-syllabic words, ample opportunity for practicing advanced word analysis skills, particularly high frequency word parts, and spelling instruction should be used to complement and reinforce word analysis in reading.

Reading fluency instruction in third grade should continue to focus on reading with attention to prosody, the smooth rhythm of language. Strategies for increasing fluency should be modeled by teachers and then practiced in materials that are interesting, at an independent level, and whenever possible the child has had a choice in selecting.

Third grade vocabulary instruction should be a continuation of the progression of skill development such that new essential words and concepts are taught explicitly, and meanings are related and discussed in children's everyday language in order to make connections between prior knowledge and new knowledge. Words and concepts targeted for instruction are selected based on usefulness, and children are given many opportunities for successful practice and regular review of vocabulary words and concepts. Children are supported in making connections between new words and known words and in processing meanings through multiple and varied exposures in order to encourage deeper level processing. Teachers may use strategies such as think-alouds to demonstrate using context to determine meaning. Vocabulary development is supported when children are helped to see the relationship and connection between words with instruction in synonyms and antonyms, with instruction in advanced word analysis, and through dictionary and thesaurus instruction. Children need to extend their vocabulary through listening (stories, informational pieces, and conversations/discussions), speaking (in class formally as in a book report or class discussion, or informally as in conversations), reading (texts at their instructional level), and writing (for a formal assignment, or an informal task).

Sometime in or about the third grade the subtle shift from learning to read, to reading to learn takes place. Reading materials become an important mechanism in how children acquire and remember information. With each year beyond the third grade this becomes more and more true. Therefore, making sure that all children have the necessary skills to comprehend content in their texts is an extremely important mission. It is essential that children know how to use a variety of strategies appropriately, with different text structures and for different purposes, so they develop efficient comprehension skills. Examples of such strategies include summarization, imagery, question generation and answering, and comprehension monitoring.

Literacy instruction for children in primary grades builds on and extends prior skill development. Instruction should be explicit and systematic and should include a cumulative review of essential skills in phonics, word analysis, and vocabulary, as well as continued development of fluency and comprehension skills. By the end of this stage (approximately third grade) the basis for future learning in the content areas is heavily related to information in textbooks. Therefore, essential skills in literacy are vitally important to a child's overall academic success. The importance of literacy development cannot be overstated. Providing children with quality literacy instruction so that they can reach their potential is giving them the gift of a literate life.

Setting up the Literacy Block

In setting up the literacy block teachers need to consider many things. First, instruction should focus on the following "big five" essential elements of literacy instruction: phonemic awareness, phonics, vocabulary, fluency, and comprehension. Next, consideration must be given to learning standards. In addition, teachers should be aware of and use evidence-based instruction— instructional practices that have been validated by reliable research—and they should use ongoing assessments to monitor progress and plan future instruction. An extended daily literacy block of at least two hours and ideally three hours allows for appropriate instructional focus, coverage, progress monitoring, and assessment. Furthermore, writing should be linked to reading on a daily basis. Instructional times should be flexible and depend on the needs of individual children, such that instruction is scaffolded and all parts are interrelated. In addition, assessment and progress monitoring should be on-going. For example, a daily schedule may include 20 to 25 minutes in whole group teacher directed instruction to set the stage for the literacy block, followed by 15 to 20 minutes of fluency work, and 30 minutes of word study. Then the rest of the literacy block could be dedicated to specific comprehension strategy work and writing. See Figures 9.3 through 9.7 for an example of how the literacy block might be organized.

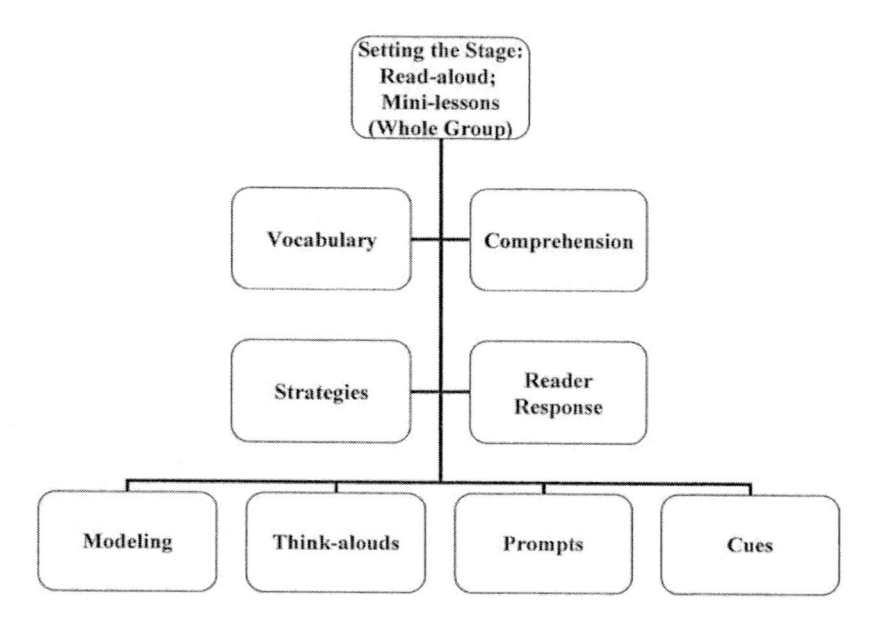

Figure 9.3. Setting the Stage in the Literacy Block.

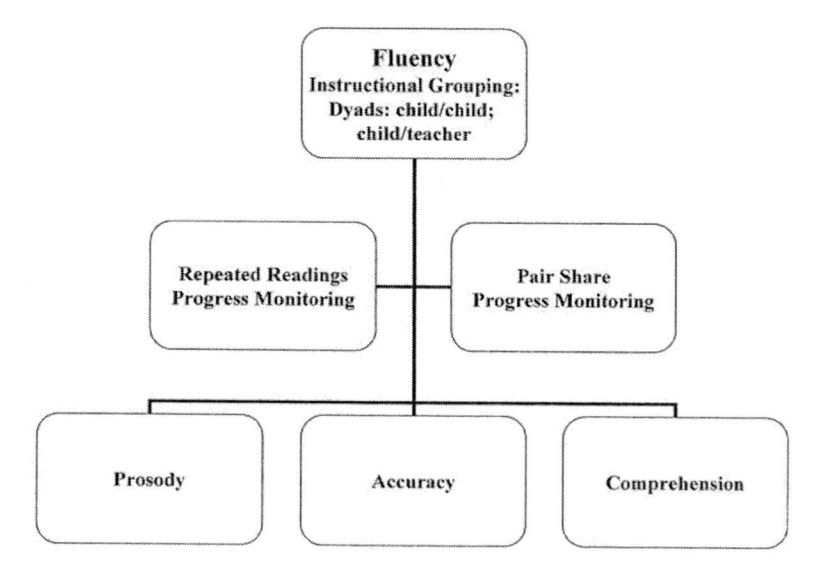

Figure 9.4. Fluency in the Literacy Block.

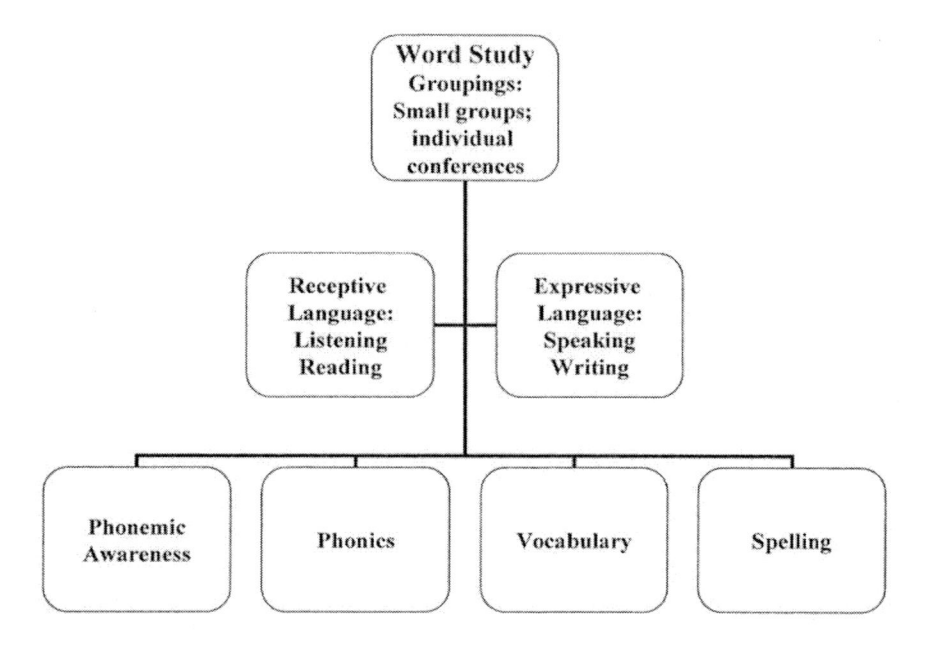

Figure 9.5. Word Study in the Literacy Block.

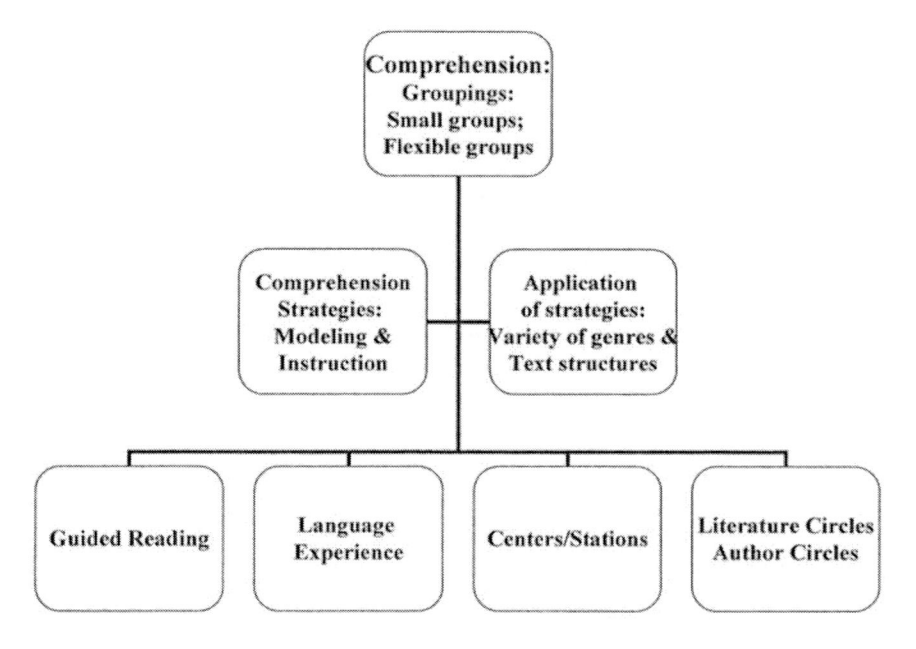

Figure 9.6. Comprehension Instruction in the Literacy Block.

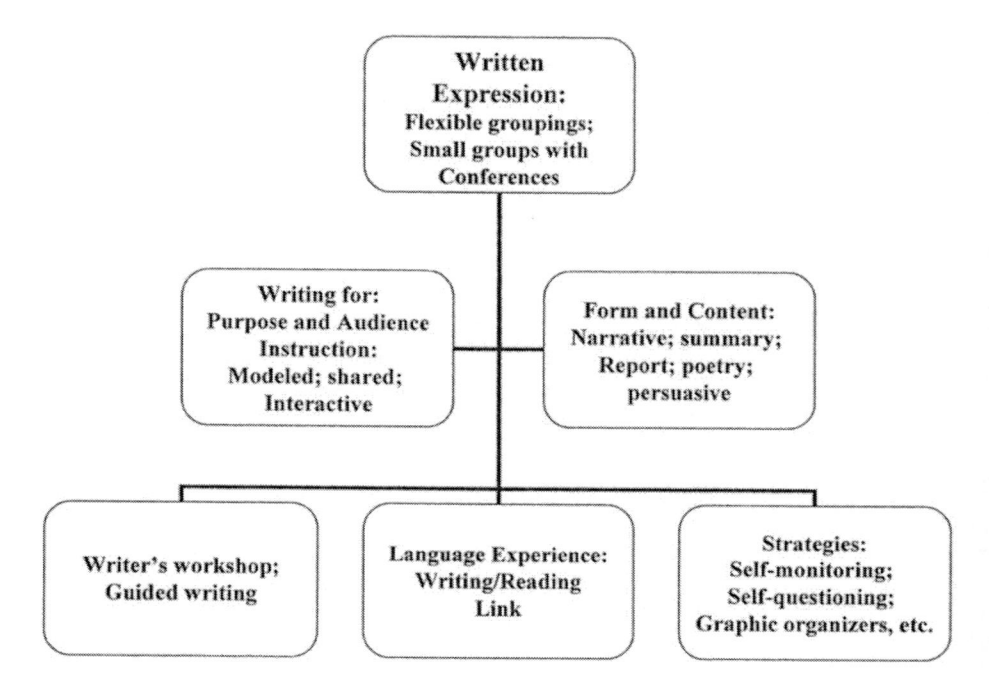

Figure 9.7. Writing in the Literacy Block.

QUESTIONS FOR REFLECTION AND DISCUSSION

1) How do you, or how will you, develop and implement reasoned and logical literacy instruction to reach each of your students?
2) Staying abreast of the current developments in literacy instruction is important. Find a current peer reviewed journal article that addresses literacy instruction that has demonstrated improvement in reading for students with disabilities. How were the students helped?

CHAPTER APPLICATION EXERCISES

1) Locate the state standards for literacy for grade 2. Create a graphic organizer to link specific state standards to the elements of phonemic awareness, phonics, vocabulary, fluency, and reading comprehension presented in the chapter.

2) Set up a daily schedule for teaching reading and writing within a 3-hour literacy block. Create a poster to illustrate your daily schedule. Be sure to indicate the time allocated for each element, the instructional grouping, the classroom set-up, and how instruction will be carried out.

Chapter 10

CHILDREN'S LITERATURE

"It is so delightfully cold," said the Snow Man, "that it makes my whole
body crackle. This is just the kind of wind to blow life into one."
(Hans Christian Andersen in The Snow Man)

What is children's literature? What qualifies as a *good* book? These two
questions may appear simple on the surface. However, actually answering them
may prove a bit more difficult. Think about what makes a book a children's book.
How does a children's book differ from other types of books? Think about your
own favorite children's books. What are the characteristics that make them your
favorites? What do you remember about the books? How did they make you feel?
Consider the emotions that can be evoked from reading a good book.

Children's literature is the term used to describe the body of books that are
read to and by children. The shear number of books in this group is incredible.
Children's books are creative works and have so much to offer both children and
adults. Oftentimes, the artwork in and of itself deserves focused attention and
appreciation. The visual aspect of children's books is one of the many ways that
children's books can touch and enhance children's lives. Good books can help
children understand the world around them. For example, children may learn
vicariously from the characters' experiences contained within stories. Books can
help children become aware of issues and the commonalities of the human
experience. Books can bring out emotions, help children develop compassion
toward others, and help children learn about a huge variety of subjects. Books can
inspire dreams and encourage imagination. Furthermore, books can be a catalyst
to open up dialogue and discussion.

Children's books are often discussed in terms of genre. A genre is simply a
category. Children's literature is typically divided into the following genres:
folktales, realistic fiction, fantasy, poetry, historical fiction, biography, and

informational. It should be noted that the divisions between the genres are not set in stone. There is some overlap. Moreover, picture books do not constitute a separate genre, but rather picture books represent a type of format (a way of presentation).

There are several qualities which are typical of books for young children. (See Figure 10.1). First, the characters are relatable in some way. The characters may be similar in age to the intended audience or they may have problems that are universal for young children. In addition, the storyline is usually straightforward and fairly uncomplicated. A linear sequence from problem to solution is common, and the story is set in one place. Another common quality of books for young children is that the language is colorful, vivid, and concrete. For example, picture books may primarily name characters and their actions, and dialogue may be used to help the story along.

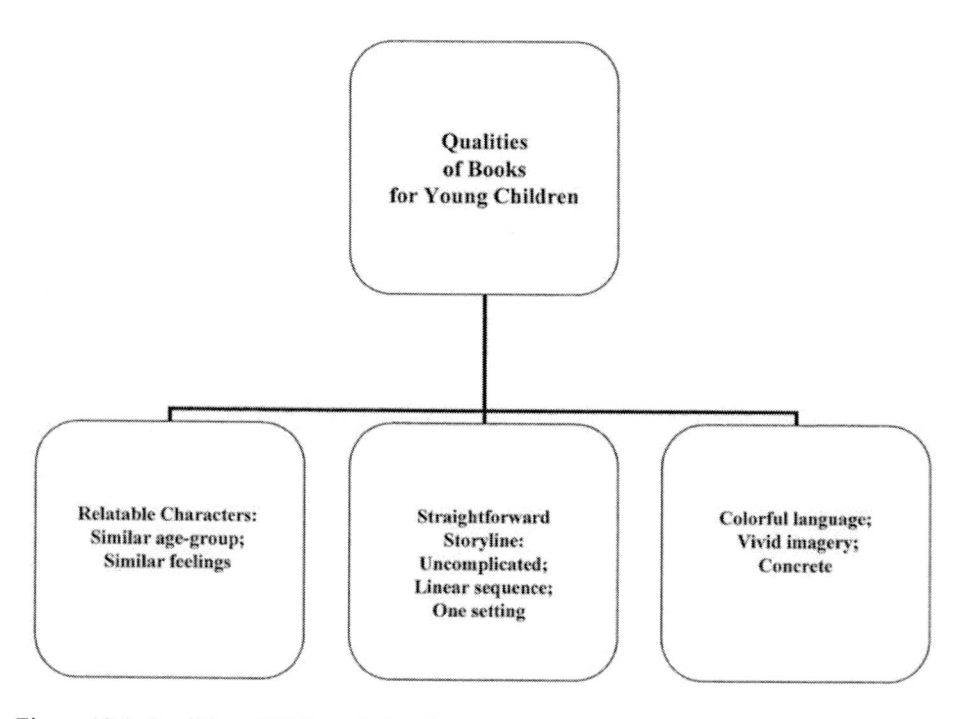

Figure 10.1. Qualities of Children's Books.

QUALITIES OF GOOD CHILDREN'S BOOKS

First, good children's books help children develop background knowledge. Reading or listening to books is one way to develop background knowledge without having to actually experience a situation directly. Children can share experiences with a character vicariously. In addition, good books help children develop their vocabularies and conceptual knowledge, yet they do not come across as contrived. Good books are enjoyable and deal with basic human truths and insights. Furthermore, good children's books use carefully selected language to convey sensory meanings (sounds and images) with believable characters and plots. Finally, good children's books help children see the world in new ways.

Books and Childhood

Reading aloud to children is beneficial in many ways. When parents read aloud to their children routinely at bedtime, a sense of tradition and that *special-time* feeling of closeness and security may be enhanced. One of the significant benefits of reading aloud to children, whether by the teacher or parent, is the exposure to and interaction with language. Young children learn the labels of objects and begin to learn related concepts through shared reading activities with adults. The give and take that occurs in reading aloud supports the child's language learning. Children also begin to learn important concepts about how books and language are related. They learn related book concepts such as covers, titles, illustrations, and the fact that what is spoken in language can be written down and read. Children also learn that books (in English) are read from front to back, top to bottom, and left to right. Through listening to stories, children also learn that stories have a grammar—a plot with characters, setting, problem and solution.

Young children in the preschool to first grade range (ages 4—7) seem to be especially interested in stories with strong plots like fairy tales and folktales that show characters that are clearly good or bad and situations that are clearly right or wrong (Temple, Martinez & Yokota, 2011). Through stories children can be guided through some of the moral dilemmas of life. At this point in their development children may not be able to focus on more than one aspect of a character's situation, but with support from a parent or teacher they begin to see more layers of a plot.

As children enter school and begin to learn to read on their own, the books they read are geared toward the words and skills they are learning. Due to the limitations in language usage, as well as the length of stories, these books may be very different from the books they have come to enjoy as active listeners in terms of plot and character development. However, there are some *easy readers* which are written with skill development in mind, yet convey rich, fun, and interesting content. Authors such as Bill Martin, Arnold Lobel, and James Marshall have written stories such that children can practice their newly acquired skills, while enjoying the content of the stories at the same time.

In children's literature, just as in adult literature, there are broad categories of writing known as fiction and nonfiction, and sub-categories known as genre. A genre has a unique set of characteristics with specific guidelines or rules. This helps readers know what to expect. The primary genres of children's literature include folktales (fairy tales, legends, fables, epics, myths), realistic fiction (adventure stories, humorous stories, relationship stories), fantasy (other-worldly or supernatural elements), poetry (works in verse), historical fiction, biography, and informational works. However, at times the boundaries between the genres seem to blur or overlap. Furthermore, it is important to realize that picture books may be written in any of the genres.

Literary Elements

The genre is one of the main literary elements. Other literary elements include setting, plot, theme, stance of the expected reader, point of view, and author's style. The setting involves the time and place of a particular story. The description of the setting is one way an author entices the reader to step into the story. Settings and their level of description vary from genre to genre. For example, folktale setting descriptions tend to include few details, but offer associations because of the customary use of terms such as home, town, country, forest, cottage, or palace. In folktales *home* is often the safe, secure place of normal life, while the *forest* is the foreboding place where something will happen. Similarly, *country* may represent the place where simple and honest people live, while *town* may indicate a place where more sophisticated but possibly unsavory characters reside.

On the other hand, the settings in realistic fiction tend to be filled with details. In realistic fiction the setting may include the character's immediate social group or family, the character's cultural group and social class, the location or geography of the setting, typical activities that occur within the setting, and the historical period of the story. Sometimes, the setting is almost a character in its own right, especially when the setting is full of problems or challenges the character must battle with or strive to overcome.

Another main literacy element is characterization. Characterization is the way in which the characters in the story come to life. Characters are introduced and described in various ways. They may be presented to readers by way of what they do (their actions), by the roles they play (protagonists, antagonists, supporting roles), by the relationships they have (who they interact with and how), by the character's voice (how the characters describe themselves), through what the characters learn or their *epiphanies,* and finally by the author's description of a character.

Skillful writers may not come out and tell the reader, but rather they may choose to show the reader. Just as in real life, children learn about other people through what they say and do. That is, authors often develop the characters in a story through their actions. In addition, characters are often brought to life through their interactions and relationships within their group, and often the characters are in conflict in some way with their group. Moreover, characters may reveal themselves through their own voice when they have and express an "ah-ha" moment of realization.

The essence of any story often comes down to a demonstration of what happened to the main character and how those events helped the character change as the story progressed. In this way stories may teach children some important life lessons without appearing to teach. Children learn through observation.

Central to any story is the plot or the organization of *who did what and why?* In general, a plot unfolds when the central character is faced with a conflict in reaching some sort of goal. The conflict could be between characters, within a character, between a character and the environment, or between a character and society. Plots have some universal structural features which include: the introduction (or exposition); the complication (introduction of conflict and characters); the rising action (characters work through complication); climax (ultimate point in which character tries to resolve conflict; point of most tension— occurs towards the end of a book); falling action (rapid series of events); denouement or resolution (tensions are relaxed). In children's literature there are several recurring plots that are used over and over again in stories. These recurring plots may help children better understand the human condition. Two recurring plots are the initiation story and the journey. The initiation story is a story plot in which a young character faces a challenge, meets the challenge which may include trade-offs (i.e., the protagonist trades innocence for experience) and is then recognized as more worthy or is accepted as having *grown up*. The initiation story is one of pain, struggle, change, and progress. Another example of a recurring plot in children's literature is the journey in which the character is compelled to make a pilgrimage, meet challenges along the way, and is forever changed in the process.

Another main literary element is the theme of a piece. A theme is the issue or lesson that is central to the work and answers the question, "What does it all mean?" Themes may be either implicit, that is not directly stated, or they may be explicit. In addition, themes may be inherent in a work, yet not intended by the author. This is true especially when considering gender, age, social class, race, and people who have disabilities.

Another element worthy of mention is the stance of the implied reader. The implied or expected reader is the person that the author imagines as the audience as he or she creates a story. In children's literature, a book may be geared toward children who are imagined as listeners or toward children who pick up a book and read independently. With the implied reader in mind the author structures the work to bring about certain desired responses—everything from excitement to humor to empathy. When actual readers respond to a story by identifying with characters, taking a moral perspective, or filling in any gaps (reader's realizations) the book successfully reaches the implied reader.

The point of view of the presentation of the story is also an important literary element. An author can use first person such that one of the characters tells the story (using first-person pronoun *I*) or the author can use third person such that a narrator outside the story tells the story (using *he, she, they*) but the narration keeps to what the characters know. An author may also use third-person omniscient (*all-knowing*) in which the author tells story events from the point of view of a narrator who is all knowing (knows more than a character could know).

Finally, style incorporates the sub-elements of word usage, visualization or imagery, metaphors, sounds, and voice. Style has to do with the craft an author uses to transport the reader to another time and place. The language used may be either simple or complex, but the author chooses words that bring the story to life. Similarly, writers often make use of images so that readers may experience the events of a story through their own senses. Writers also use metaphors to talk about something in terms of another. A metaphor is often used to help get across a concept that may not be familiar. Another important sub-component of style is the way in which the sounds of language are used in the writing—the flow and the rhythm of the text. Lastly, the voice is the tone of the author. The voice may be relaxed, informal, knowledgeable, strong, and so forth. The voice of a story reflects the personality, world-view, and dialect of the narrator. In sum, all these sub-elements contribute to the author's style.

PICTURE BOOKS

Picture books are a format for the presentation of a children's book rather than a genre. That is, a picture book may be in the genre of realistic fiction, fantasy, historical fiction, poetry, and so forth. There are picture books that are early childhood books (toy books including pop-ups, tactile, and even sense of smell books, board, and cloth books), picture books that are storybooks, picture books that are concept books (shapes, colors, alphabet, and counting books), wordless picture books, and picture books that are beginning readers. In any case, picture books rely on the art within to either help convey or solely convey the story or message. In short, picture books are works of art to be appreciated and enjoyed over and over again. Picture storybooks include books in which the text and pictures work together—part of the story is told through pictures and part of the story is told through the text. Picture storybooks are the most prevalent type of picture book. They have characteristically rich language and are usually good for read-alouds. Figures 10.2 through 10.5 include examples of a variety of types of picture books.

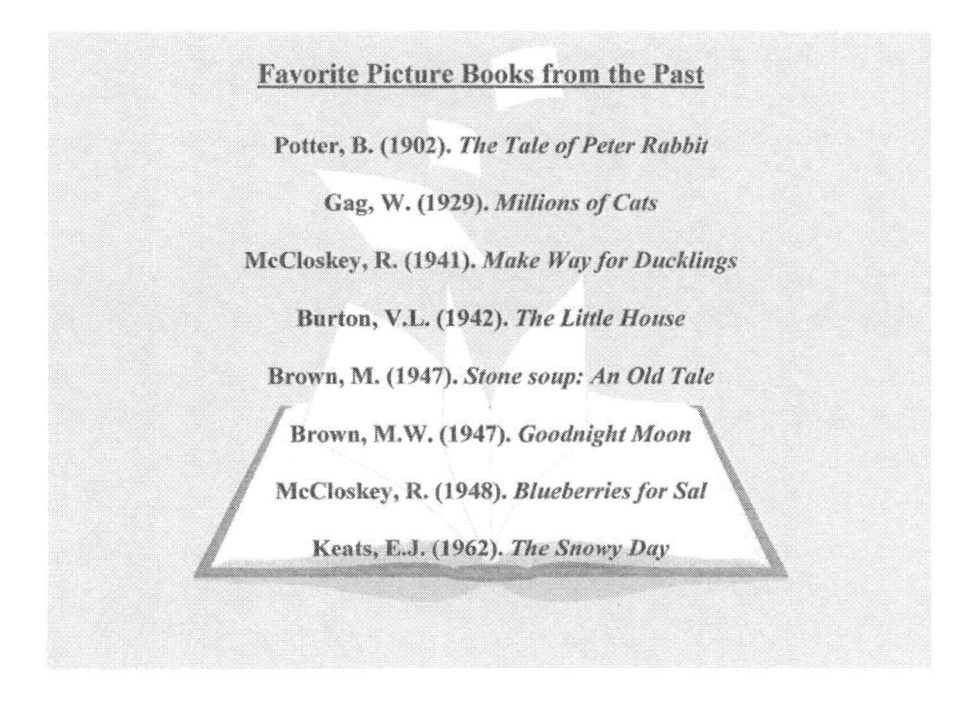

Favorite Picture Books from the Past

Potter, B. (1902). *The Tale of Peter Rabbit*

Gag, W. (1929). *Millions of Cats*

McCloskey, R. (1941). *Make Way for Ducklings*

Burton, V.L. (1942). *The Little House*

Brown, M. (1947). *Stone soup: An Old Tale*

Brown, M.W. (1947). *Goodnight Moon*

McCloskey, R. (1948). *Blueberries for Sal*

Keats, E.J. (1962). *The Snowy Day*

Figure 10.2. Picture Books: Favorites from the Past.

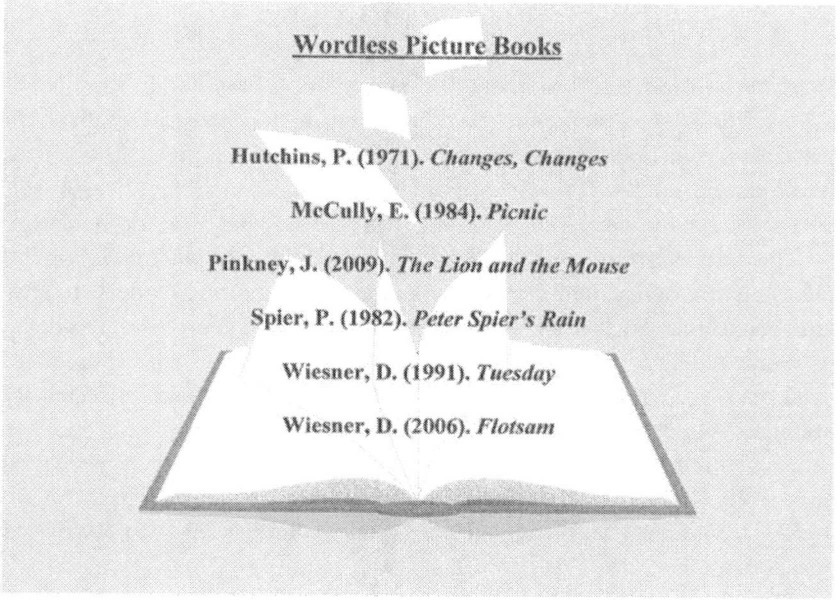

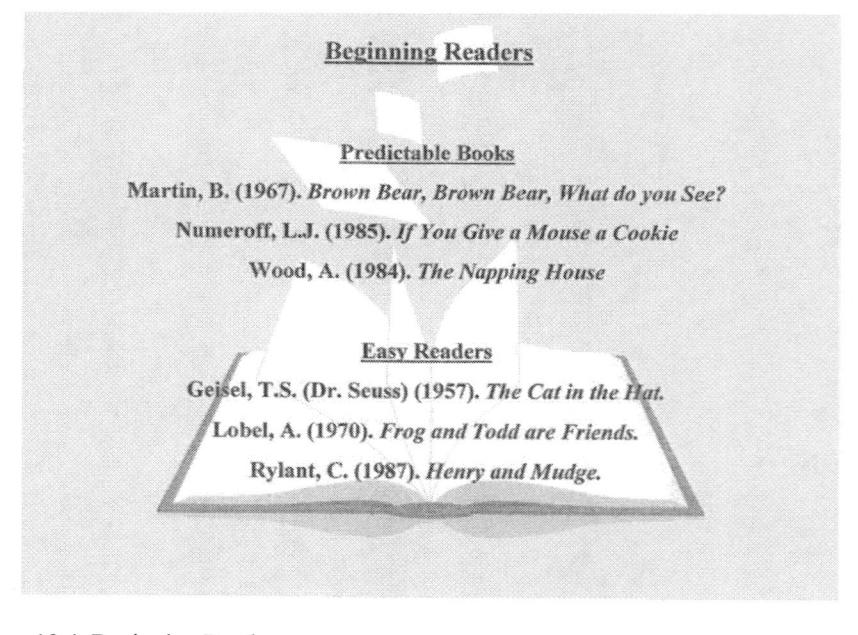

Wordless Picture Books

Hutchins, P. (1971). *Changes, Changes*

McCully, E. (1984). *Picnic*

Pinkney, J. (2009). *The Lion and the Mouse*

Spier, P. (1982). *Peter Spier's Rain*

Wiesner, D. (1991). *Tuesday*

Wiesner, D. (2006). *Flotsam*

Figure 10.3. Wordless Picture Books.

Beginning Readers

Predictable Books

Martin, B. (1967). *Brown Bear, Brown Bear, What do you See?*

Numeroff, L.J. (1985). *If You Give a Mouse a Cookie*

Wood, A. (1984). *The Napping House*

Easy Readers

Geisel, T.S. (Dr. Seuss) (1957). *The Cat in the Hat.*

Lobel, A. (1970). *Frog and Todd are Friends.*

Rylant, C. (1987). *Henry and Mudge.*

Figure 10.4. Beginning Readers.

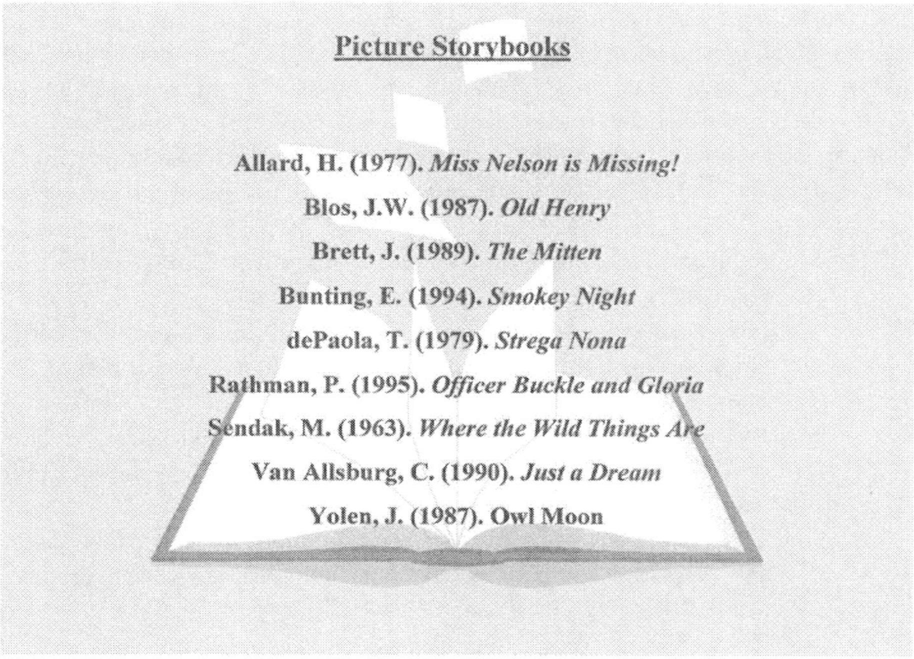

Picture Storybooks

Allard, H. (1977). *Miss Nelson is Missing!*

Blos, J.W. (1987). *Old Henry*

Brett, J. (1989). *The Mitten*

Bunting, E. (1994). *Smokey Night*

dePaola, T. (1979). *Strega Nona*

Rathman, P. (1995). *Officer Buckle and Gloria*

Sendak, M. (1963). *Where the Wild Things Are*

Van Allsburg, C. (1990). *Just a Dream*

Yolen, J. (1987). Owl Moon

Figure 10.5. Picture Storybooks.

Children's Picture Books and the Elements of Design

In a picture book, the elements of design (line, shape, light, color, and texture) are critically important and impact how well a story or message is communicated. For example, line can be used to indicate distance and movement; shape can be used to indicate solidness, distance, and space; color can be used to give contrast and focus; light can be used to highlight or indicate the time of day; and texture can be used to give depth and contrast in an illustration. In combination these elements make up the composition of the artwork. Children need support and scaffolding in learning to interpret the visual elements of a work.

Artists use various media in children's books. These media range from paints (watercolor, gouache, acrylic, oil), to pen and pencil drawings, to photography, to three dimensional mixed media, to block printing (woodcut, linoleum cut), to scratchboard, to computer generated art.

The artistic style of an illustration is the term used to describe the overall effect of the way the visual elements are used (line, shape, color, light, texture).

The artistic style is what helps create mood, the context for the story, define characters, and should work in concert with the text. The most common artistic styles found in children's literature include realism, impressionism, expressionism, surrealism, romanticism, folk art, naïve art, abstract, and post modern. Sometimes children's books contain the elements of more than one artistic style, and some illustrators have their own unique personal style.

- Realism: Realistic portrayal, accurate, often with a portrait-like quality (e.g., Allen Say, *Grandfather's Journey*).
- Impressionism: Less restrictive and defined lines, more interpretive, emphasis on light and color and motion (e.g., Jerry Pinkney, *The Lion and the Mouse*).
- Expressionism: Emphasis on feeling and mood, emphasis given to aspects of an illustration through proportion, placement, and more detail (e.g., David Shannon, *Encounter*).
- Surrealism: The artist uses unexpected elements to stir imagination and express internal feelings or thoughts, or even represent symbolism (e.g., Chris Van Allsburg, *The Dream*).
- Romanticism: World depicted as enchanted with rich colorful pictures; almost glowing quality; soft, round, flowing images; intricate details (e.g., Kate Greenaway, *Mother Goose*).
- Folk Art: Used to depict culture and time and place with unique symbols, colors, designs; may have primitive quality; helps reader understand setting (e.g., Donald Hall, Barbara Cooney illustrator, *Ox-Cart Man*).
- Naïve Art: Child-like in form; flat and two dimensional (e.g., Vera Williams, *A Chair for my Mother*).
- Abstract Art: Images are not accurate, rather they are altered; shape and color used to evoke images and represent feelings (e.g., Yumi Heo, *The Green Frogs: A Korean Folktale*).
- Cartoon: Playful, lively, fast-paced action; proportion may be exaggerated for emphasis; line may be used to indicate emotions (e.g., Peggy Rathmann, *Officer Buckle and Gloria*).
- Postmodern: Breaks with traditional art; may have disorder or discontinuity; reader has to make sense of illustrations (use of background knowledge) (e.g., Weisner, *The Three Pigs*).

Visual Communication in Picture Books

Visual communication is a term used to describe the visual elements of a picture book that contribute to comprehension or contribute to the book's effect. These include the book's design (including size, shape, layout, cover, etc.), visual consistency of characters, setting, perspective, background, color, and the interaction of text and image.

The pictures in a children's book work together with the text to create a whole, congruous, interrelated work. Everything from the size and shape of the book to how the illustrations are placed within the book (single pages, double-page spread) has an impact on the reader's response and how they move through the book (steady pacing vs. pausing to examine a double-page spread). The cover of the book, because it is the first thing a child sees, is a visual invitation to the book, while the last page of a picture book is often an epilogue of sorts. As the journey through a picture book unfolds, color and light are often used to depict mood and emotion. Specific colors and the intensity of colors may be used to communicate a mood. However, it is also possible to depict mood in black and white illustrations through the use of shading, by controlling the amount of white space, and by varying the intensity and boldness of lines. In addition, shading and crosshatching may be used to indicate depth and texture.

Picture books are evaluated according to how well the text and pictures combine to communicate together. Quality picture books are well written, well-crafted, incorporate illustrations that communicate to the reader through color, light, texture, etc., and integrate pictures and text so that they enhance each other. There are many awards to honor excellence in children's picture books. The oldest award for picture book illustrators, the Caldecott, was established in 1938 and is an annual award given by the American Library Association. The Corretta Scott King Award, also given by the ALA, is given to African American illustrators and authors to honor distinguished works that promote appreciation of culture. In addition, the Charlotte Zolotow Award honors excellence in picture book text, and the Theodor Seuss Geisel Award is given to honor beginning reader books. The following are just a sampling of some of today's important picture book authors and illustrators:

- Eric Carle: *The Very Hungry Caterpillar, The Grouchy Ladybug, The Very Hungry, Spider, The Very Quiet Cricket, The Art of Eric Carle*
- Kevin Henkes: *Kitten's First Full Moon, Wemberly Worried, Chrysanthemum, Lilly's Purple Plastic Purse*

- Jerry Pinkney: *The Patchwork Quilt, Mirandy and Brother Wind, Half a Moon and One Whole Star, The Ugly Duckling, The Lion and the Mouse*
- Maurice Sendak: *Where the Wild Things Are; The Nutshell Library(a set of four tiny books—Chicken Soup with Rice: A Book of Months; One Was Johnny: A Counting Book; Alligators All Around: An Alphabet; and Pierre: A Cautionary Tale).*
- William Steig: *Sylvester and the Magic Pebble, The Amazing Bone, Doctor De Soto, Pete's a Pizza*
- Chris Van Allsburg: *The Garden of Abdul Gasazi, Jumanji, The Polar Express, Just a Dream*
- David Wiesner: *Free Fall, Tuesday, June 29, 1999, The Three Pigs, Flotsam*

DIVERSITY AND MULTICULTURALISM

The United States is a diverse society, and children's literature is one way to help children understand others' points of view. Diversity includes the many ways that people differ from one another and often includes gender, ethnic and racial background, language, exceptionalities in cognitive and physical functioning, and even social class. Children's literature is one way for children to explore the experiences and emotions of someone who is different from them in some way. In addition, books can function as an introduction to discussions of related issues such as social justice.

The degree to which a book highlights diversity differs greatly. In some stories diversity may be highlighted and central to the story, such that the reader is given an opportunity to experience differences in the ways the characters live their lives (values, beliefs, attitudes, language, etc.) compared to how they experience their own lives. On the other hand, in other stories diversity is only an incidental part of the story. That is, the theme is generic to any culture (the theme does not necessitate that the characters come from any particular group) and demonstrates the commonalities of experiences across cultures. Both types of stories are important for children to experience.

The following questions should be kept in mind when deciding on the appropriateness of a work.

- Does the book depict diversity (culture, exceptionality, gender, etc.) in an authentic way?
- Which group is described in the book?
- Does the work promote any stereotypes? (e.g., a person with a disability as a victim).
- Does the author write from an inside or an outside perspective?

The following is a list of some important multicultural authors and illustrators:

- Alma Flor Ada: *Tales our Abuelitas Told: A Hispanic Folktale Collection; The Gold Coin; My Name is Maria Isabel/Me Llamo Maria Isabel: Under the Royal Palms: A Childhood in Cuba*
- Joseph Bruchac: *The First Strawberries: A Cherokee Story; A Boy Called Slow; Eagle Song; In the Heart; Bowman's Store*
- Ashley Bryan: *The Dancing Granny; Beautiful Blackbird; Beat the Story-Drum; Lion and the Ostrich Chicks and Other African Folk Tales*
- Virginia Hamilton: *M.C. Higgins, the Great; The Planet of Junior Brown; Sweet Whispers, Brother Rush; Her Stories; The People Could Fly: American Black Folktales; Anthony Burns: The Defeat and Triumph of a Fugitive Slave*
- Walter Dean Myers: *Harlem; Patrol; Blues Journey*
- Allen Say: *Grandfather's Journey; Tea with Milk; Tree of Cranes; The Boy of the Three-Year Nap*
- Gary Soto: *Baseball in April and Other Stories; Too Many Tamales; Chato's Kitchen*

The following authors and books portray nontraditional gender roles:

- Katherine Patereson: *The King's Equal*
- Rachel Isadora: *Max*
- Betsy Hearne: *Seven Brave Women*
- Joanna Cole: *Magic School Bus (series)*

The following authors and books portray social unrest:

- Eve Bunting: *Smokey Night*
- Minfong Ho: *The Clay Marble*

The following authors and books portray social and economic diversity:

- Barbara Dugan: *Loop the Loop*
- Rosemarie Hausherr: *Celebrating Families*
- Katherine Paterson: *The Flip Flop Girl*

The following authors and books portray learners with exceptionalities:

- Virgina Fleming: *Be Good to Eddie Lee*
- Lisa Rowe Fraustino: *The Hickory Chair*
- Ann Martin: *A Corner of the Universe*
- Patricia Polacco: *Thank you, Mr. Falker*

POETRY

Poetry is considered an artful use of language that invites readers and listeners to pause, appreciate, examine, ponder, and reflect. Poems may have a rhythm; they may rhyme; they may be visually arranged on the page; and they often focus on pleasing sounds. Poetry can take many forms (haiku, sonnet, etc.,) and have many classifications (nursery rhymes, folk poems, lyric or expressive poems, narrative poems, etc.). For example, the familiar childhood nursery rhymes often have accompanying movements that go along with the words (e.g., *This Little Piggy*). The category of lyric or expressive poetry includes poems that express the author's insights and emotions, and poems in this category may not follow a recognized form. Free verse does not have a recognizable rhyme or rhythm, but creates its flow with the intensity of feelings presented. One type of poem with a distinguishable format is the Haiku poem. Haiku poems are usually about nature and traditionally contain a first line with five syllables, a second line with seven syllables, and a final line with five syllables. On the other hand, narrative poems tell a story. One example of a children's narrative poem is Clement C. Moore's *T'was the Night Before Christmas*. Another poetry classification, nonsense verse, is often humorous in content and many children enjoy listening and reading this type of poetry. Finally, dialogue poems are written for two or more voices and are meant to be read aloud. The essential qualities that contribute to good poetry include the sounds, the images, and the forms. Included in sound are the sub-elements of rhythm (the beat), rhyme (the musicality), and alliteration (the repetition of sounds), and onomatopoeia (the imitation of sounds—moo, clang). An author creates images with words by appealing to the senses, thereby helping the child experience how things look, sound, smell, feel, and taste. The form of a poem or the arrangement of the words on a page affects the how quickly the reader moves through the poem, how much emphasis is given to particular words, and sometimes the arrangement is done to represent the subject of the poem (a concrete poem). Children seem to especially enjoy poetry that contain rhymes and rhythm, are funny, and contain familiar experiences and animals such as the work of Jack Prelutsky and Shel Silverstein. However, children's tastes in poetry should be expanded with exposure through activities such as read alouds, and performances. For example, John Ciardi's *You Read to Me, I'll Read to You* may be used as a read-aloud, and Paul Fleischman's *Big Talk: Poems for Fours Voices* may be used as a performance piece.

TRADITIONAL LITERATURE: FOLKTALES, FAIRY TALES, LEGENDS, AND MYTHS

Traditional literature is the genre that is made up of memorable stories that have been passed down through the generations orally, and the original authors are unknown. Fairy tales are one type of folktale, and they are characterized by the inclusion of something otherworldly or extraordinary. Folktales offer children insights into universal human themes, encourage children's imagination, and offer an introduction to many other cultures. In addition, folktales have strong plots, and present characters who are easily defined as good or bad.

The setting for most folktales is rather vague in comparison to contemporary stories. In the very first sentence of a folktale, children are cued that the story that follows is fictional, perhaps even otherworldly. This helps children get ready to listen and "believe" if only for a little while. Sometimes this process is referred to as suspending disbelief. For example, the opening phrase, "Once upon a time...," prepares children for something extraordinary to follow. Generally, the settings of folktales are very basic and specific places have significance. For example, cottages are where the common folk live, and castles are the places where people live when their dreams come true. Folktales take on such themes as honesty, perseverance, ambition, and greed. The characters in folktales take on roles that they play out in the story (hero, villain, helper, rival, etc.). The roles that the characters play define them. The plots in folktales tend to stand out for a couple reasons. First, folktales are relatively short so the plot has to unfold quickly. Second, plots are more upfront and center because they are familiar plots. This is due to the fact that folktale patterns of events are often variations of the same plots which occur in many different folktales around the world. According to Joseph Campbell (1989) in *The Power of Myth*, traditional literatures of many cultures often present the same tale. For example, in a hero tale there is a similar unfolding of events that leads to a young person's coming-of-age (symbolic for young people), the rediscovery of life's meaning (symbolic for middle age people), and a review of the path taken (symbolic for older people).

The following are some considerations to keep in mind when thinking about traditional literature selections for use in the classroom:

- Is the tale well-written?
- Does the author's retelling the tale identify (give proper credit) for the origin of the story and note any significant changes from the original?
- Does the tale give children insight into how others (from other cultures) live and how they think?

The following list includes examples of traditional children's literature and their culture of origin:

- Alma Flor Ada's *The Gold Coin* (Hispanic)
- Jim Aylesworth's *The Gingerbread Man* (Great Britain)
- Joseph Bruchac's *The First Strawberries: A Cherokee Story* (Native American)
- Demi's *The Donkey and the Rock* (Asian)
- Cherry Gilchrist's *Prince Ivan and the Firebird* (Russian)
- William Hooks' *Moss Gown* (America)
- Anne Isaacs' *Swamp Angel, Paul Bunyan, Pecos Bill* (America)
- Paul Galdone's *The Little Red Hen* (Great Britain, Hansel and Gretel (German)
- Steven Kellogg's *The Three Sillies* (Great Britain)
- Anthony Manna's and Chris Mitakidou's *Mr. Semolina Semolinus: A Greek Folktale*

- Gerald McDermott's *Coyote: A Trickster Tale from the American Southwest* (Native American); *Anansi the Spider* (African)
- P.J. Lynch's *East O' the Sun and West O' the Moon* (Scandinavian)
- Robert San Souci's *The Talking Eggs* (African American)
- Meilo So's *Gobble, Gobble, Slip, Slop: A Tale of a Very Greedy Cat* (Asian)
- John Steptoe's *Mufaro's Beautiful Daughters* (African)
- Simms Taback's *Joseph Had a Little Overcoat* (Jewish)
- Jeanette Winter's *Follow the Drinking Gourd* (African American)

In addition, there are other genres included under the umbrella of children's literature such as historical fiction, biography, and informational books that are worthy of exploration and use in the classroom.

QUESTIONS FOR REFLECTION AND DISCUSSION

1) What was your favorite book as a child? Reflect on why you consider it a favorite. Write your recollections in a one page journal entry.
2) What elements of children's books do you most enjoy as an adult? Why?
3) What makes a book a good children's book?

CHAPTER APPLICATION EXERCISES

1) Arrange to do a read-aloud for a group of children. This may be a class, an after-school program, or a small group at the local library. As you prepare for the read-aloud consider the following:

   a) Determine a purpose for sharing the book.
   b) Make sure the author's style and language are appropriate for the children's ages and interests.
   c) Consider whether the plot is appealing and the theme relevant to children's lives.
   d) Consider the illustrations and how they enhance (or not) the story elements.

e) Conduct the read-aloud and then write a reflection about it. What went well? What would you change the next time you do a read-aloud?

2) Locate several books that you believe portray individuals with disabilities in realistic ways. Prepare a book talk and share these books with others.

Chapter 11

WRITING CONVENTIONS

When it comes right down to it, nothing has changed. The English sentence
is just as difficult to write as it ever was.
(John Steinbeck)

WORD CHOICE

Receptive vocabulary comprehension in reading and listening, and expressive vocabulary usage in writing and speaking are related skills. Not only is vocabulary development one of the building blocks of efficient reading, vocabulary development also plays a vital role in the development of written expression skills. However, the fact that someone has a large vocabulary does not automatically insure that he or she will use that vocabulary appropriately in writing tasks. Similar to other literacy skills vocabulary or word choice in writing is an acquired skill that takes practice. Teachers should help children see the importance of word choice and should model examples of how word choice can improve communication between speaker and listener and writer and reader.

For example, when writers or speakers use care in their selection of words— when they use the exact word—they are more likely to convey a precise meaning so that the listener or reader is able to receive the intended message. Writers can also use a variety of words to clarify their intended meaning. Adjectives offer preciseness, verbs provide action and richness, and adverbs can give vividness to expression. Not only can word choice promote clarity, word choice can also make the message more interesting.

Another strategy to help make the message more interesting is to avoid overused words. Teachers can model and help children find new words for the ones they typically use. Doing so will also help improve their vocabulary skills. Teachers should encourage and teach dictionary skills. Dictionaries often give sample contexts to illustrate how to use a word. Children should also be encouraged to use a thesaurus to find synonyms for overworked words.

TEACH DICTIONARY SKILLS

Dictionary use can be an invaluable tool for the writer. Therefore, it is essential that children learn how to use one early in their educational careers. Not only does a dictionary give the correct spelling and meaning(s) for words, but a dictionary also includes information on the pronunciation of words, appropriate usage, and history. Dictionary skills are illustrated in Table 11.1.Since dictionaries differ in their format or arrangement of information, it is always a good idea to read the introductory section of a particular dictionary prior to using it in order to comprehend the information presented and get the most benefit.

Table 11.1. Dictionary Skills

Entry word: The word to be defined
How words are listed: Listed in alphabetical order
Abbreviations: Entries based on the letters in them,   not the words they stand for
Two or more words presented together (prime minister):   Treated as a single word
Opening a dictionary and locating a word   Think of dictionary in thirds (i.e., abcde; fghijklmnop; qrstuvwxyz)
Open to the third in which the word appears; then find the letter
Use the guide words at the top of the page: Left guide word is first on page;   Right guide word is last on page
More than one spelling—the first one listed is the preferred spelling
Pronunciation of words: Comes immediately after the entry word: Enclosed within   parentheses or slant bars   Indicated with phonetic respelling and symbols (a key is   usually included in the front pages of the dictionary)

Table 11.1. (Continued)

Accent marks show primary and sometimes secondary emphasis within multi-syllable words
Diacritical marks: Long vowel sounds: macron—a long straight line over the vowel Short vowel sounds: breve—a cup-shaped symbol over the vowel
Schwa: an upside-down e to represent the unclear vowel sound in unaccented syllables
Syllable division: Syllable knowledge may help spelling Small dots or dashes indicate syllable divisions
How to find the correct meaning: Scan all meanings (definitions are numbered) Examples often provide context Illustrations may show (in addition to a definition) Part of speech is indicated (adv., n., adj., v., etc.) Some dictionaries provide definitions by the part of speech Focus on the meaning with the closest fit

Since vocabulary development plays a vital role in the development of written expression skills, in addition to having self-help tools such as dictionary skills, it is essential that children are given plenty of opportunities to practice using their ever-expanding vocabularies in their developing writing skills.

WORD USAGE

The way in which words are used in sentences is vital to comprehension. One important aspect of word usage is subject and verb agreement. Closely related words should agree in form. For example, subjects and verbs should agree in number. This means that when a word refers to one person, place, idea, or thing, it is singular, and when it refers to more than one, the word is plural in number. Therefore, if a subject is singular, the verb must be singular. Likewise, if a subject is plural, the verb must be plural. It is important to remember that the subject number (singular or plural) does not change when the subject is followed by a prepositional phrase. Figure 11.1 shows an example of a classroom reminder chart for subject and verb agreement.

Subjects and Verbs Agree in Number

★ Single subjects take single verbs
★ Plural subjects take plural verbs
★ Subject number is not changed by a prepositional phrase that follows the subject
★ Singular common pronouns take singular verbs: *each, either, neither, one, everyone, everybody, no one, nobody, anyone, anybody, someone, somebody*
★ Plural common pronouns take plural verbs: *both, few, several, many*
★ Subjects joined by *and* (compound subjects that name more than one person, place, idea, thing) are plural and take a plural verb
★ Singular subjects joined by *or* or *nor:* take a singular verb
★ Collective nouns may be either singular or plural: *assembly, audience, class, club, crowd, family, flock, group, team*
★ Plural verb when noun refers to individual members or parts
★ Singular verb when noun refers to the group as a unit
★ Contractions *here's* and *there's* contain the verb *is* and should be used only with singular subjects
★ Use *don't* and *doesn't* must agree with their subjects
★ Use *don't* with plural subjects and with the pronouns *I* and *you*
★ Use *doesn't* with other subjects

Figure 11.1. Subject and Verb Agreement.

Verb tense shows the time of action. When changing from present tense to past tense not all verbs follow a regular pattern. There are some variations. Table 11.2 presents examples of present tense and past tense verb pairs.

FORMING PAST TENSE

In written expression it is better to stay consistent with tense. Keeping a consistent tense helps the reader follow the ideas and comprehend more easily. Therefore, it is a good idea to teach children not to shift tense, especially within a sentence. This concept may take quite a bit of practice and experience.

Pronouns are words that stand for nouns. Pronouns may be a subject in a sentence (e.g., I, he, she, it, you, we, they); an object (e.g., me, him, her, it, you, us, them); or they may be used to show possession (e.g., my, mine, his, hers, your, yours, our, ours, their, theirs). Pronoun errors commonly occur with compound subjects. Therefore, teachers should model how to test the pronoun by itself with the verb to determine the correct form.

Modifiers are words, phrases, and clauses that are used to define or make meaning more obvious. They also make communication more interesting, whether in speaking or writing. Table 11.3 lists examples of modifiers.

Table 11.2. Present and Past Tense

Past Tense: Action has occurred
Regular verbs: ed or d added to present form
Irregular verbs: Vowel change, consonant change, vowel and Consonant change, no change Begin, began; blow, blew; break, broke; bring, brought; burst, burst; choose, chose; come, came; do, did; drink, drank; drive, drove; eat, ate; fall, fell; freeze, froze; give, gave; go, went; know, knew; lie, lay; ride, rode; ring, rang; rise, rose; run, ran; see, saw; set, set; shrink, shrank; sing, sang; sit, sat; speak, spoke; steal, stole; swim, swam; take, took; throw, threw; write, wrote
Sit, set; lie, lay; and rise, raise Sit means to rest in an upright position (sit, sat); set means to place something (set, set) and may have an object Lie means to rest in a reclining position (lie, lay), lay means to place something down (lay, laid) and may have an object Rise means to go up (rise, rose), raise means to lift up (raise, raised) and may have an object

Table 11.3. Modifiers

Adjectives modify nouns or pronouns
Adverbs modify verbs, adjectives, or adverbs
Good and well Good: modifies a noun or pronoun Well: modifies a verb (Well: used as a adjective when referring to a person's health or appearance)
Degrees of comparison: Comparative: Comparing two things Superlative: Comparing three or more things Regular: To form the comparative and superlative versions of a word: er or est may be added, or the word more or most may precede it (e.g., weak, weaker, weakest; loudly, more loudly, most loudly) When in doubt—teach children to use a dictionary Words are compared in only one way (i.e., do not add er and also use more)

In addition to the examples in Table 11.3, the words *less* or *least* are used before a modifier to indicate less or least of a quality (e.g., less skillful, least skillful), and many modifiers have irregular forms and need to be learned as exceptions. These examples include: bad, worse, worst; good, better, best; well, better, best; many, more, most; and much, more, most. Children may learn from listening to and reading academic language to avoid double negatives. That is, only one negative word (no, not, none, never, no one, nothing, hardly, scarcely) is acceptable in one statement. However, they may use and hear double negatives often in everyday conversation. Therefore, instruction is needed to clear up any confusion.

WRITING AND GRAMMAR

Literacy may be viewed as having four vital parts that work in concert. These parts are listening, speaking, reading, and writing. Listening and reading are receptive language skills, while speaking and writing are expressive language skills. Writing is perhaps the most complex of these vital parts of literacy. Nonetheless, the ability to express oneself in writing is an important component of becoming literate. Writing is not a natural skill, but rather one that requires modeling, scaffolding, practice, trial and error, and refinement. Essential skills can be taught, learned, and developed. As with any type of content, it is important that teachers have a deep knowledge or understanding of the writing process and are proficient in the writing skills they will be teaching. What are these essential skills?

What is quality writing? Knowledge of the mechanics (capitalization, spelling, and punctuation), grammar, usage, and composition (syntax, vocabulary, text types, and organization) are just a few of the essential skills that contribute to quality written expression. What follows is a review of some of the essential skills and knowledge with which teachers must be proficient.

Spoken language and written language differ in that the writer must convey meaning through words and punctuation without the benefit of voice, volume, pace, and pausing, etc. Therefore the writer's thought units must be presented to his/her audience (the reader) through the use of complete sentences with clear punctuation.

GRAMMAR REVIEW

Teachers must be familiar with grammar in order to provide comprehensive instruction. Instruction that includes teacher modeling, systematic and explicit instruction in specific skills, many opportunities for guided practice and application, cumulative review, and many opportunities for real writing is recommended. Therefore, the following will be a review of the basics of grammar. This review is based on the work of Nunan, Griffith, and Lee (1965).

One of the most important structures of grammar is the sentence. The sentence is defined as a group of words expressing a complete thought (i.e., a syntactic unit) which expresses an assertion, a question, a command, an exclamation, and begins with a capital letter and ends with an appropriate end mark (Mish, 1994). When teaching writing to children, it is helpful to have them read their writing aloud to help determine whether or not a group of words expresses a complete thought. The term sentence base refers to the idea that in order to express a complete thought (a sentence), a group of words must have a subject and predicate (verb or action).

The subject is the part or focus of a sentence about which something is being written. The subject is often the "what" or the "who" of the sentence. In addition, a simple subject is the main word of the subject, while a complete subject includes the main word and the other words that go along with the main word. On the other hand, the predicate is the term that refers to the part of a sentence which says something about the subject. It answers the questions: What happened? What was said about the subject? A simple predicate is the verb (may be one word or several words), while the complete predicate includes the verb or verb phrase and the other words that go along with the verb. Subjects and verbs can also be compound. In other words, a compound subject has two or more subjects joined by "and" or "or", and they have the same verb. Similarly, a compound verb is two or more verbs joined by "and", "or", or "but" and, they have the same subject.

One early skill that deserves instructional attention involves the categorization of the various types of sentences. Sentences are classified based on their purpose as illustrated in Figure 11.2.

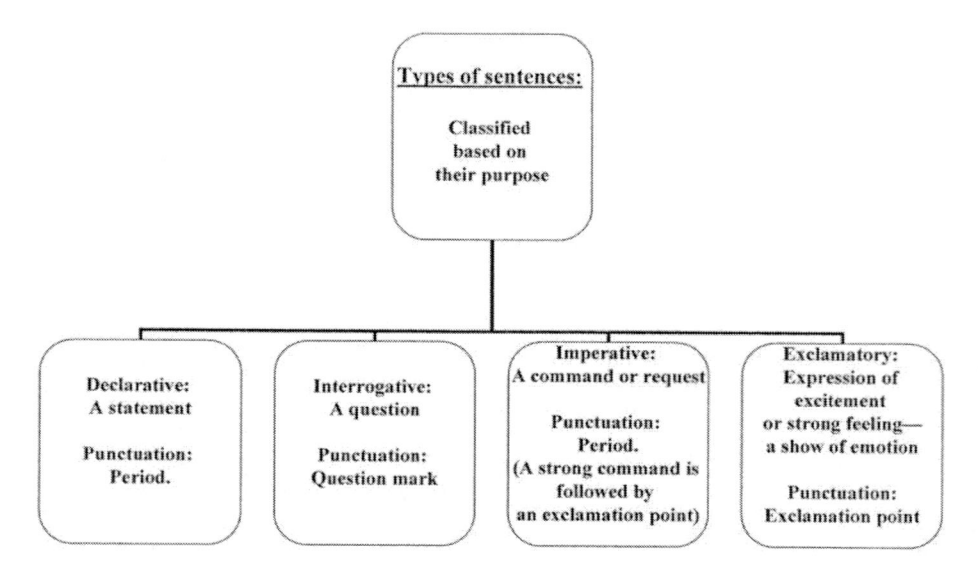

Figure 11.2. Types of Sentences.

Children need explicit instruction, modeling, and practice constructing the various types of sentences in authentic writing. In addition, instruction should include work with the parts of speech. It is important to note that the way a word is used in a sentence ultimately determines its part of speech. The parts of speech include nouns, pronouns, adjectives, verbs, adverbs, prepositions, conjunctions, and interjections. Nouns are words that are used to name a person, place, thing, or idea. A compound noun is a noun made up of two or more words, and a proper noun names a particular person, place, or thing and is capitalized.

A pronoun is a word that stands for a noun. Examples of personal pronouns include the following: *I, me, mine, my, myself, you, your, yours, yourself, yourselves, he, him, his, himself, she, her, hers, herself, it, its, itself, we, us, our, ours, ourselves, they, them, their, theirs, themselves.* Other common pronouns include the following words: *who, whom, whoever, whomever, everybody, everyone, someone, somebody, no one, nobody, none, others.* In addition, when used in the place of a noun the following words also function as pronouns: *what, which, whatever, whichever, whose, this, that, these, those, one, each, every, some, any, many, more, much, most, both, several, few, all, other, another, either, neither.*

Adjectives are words that describe or define a noun or pronoun, and they often answer one of the following: What kind? Which one? How many? How much? A special kind of adjective, called a proper adjective, is formed from a proper noun and is capitalized (e.g., American cheese, Hawaiian dance).

Verbs carry the action in sentences. An action verb is a word used to express action (physical or mental). On the other hand, a linking verb links its subject with a noun or adjective in the predicate and is often a form of the verb "be" (e.g., am, is, are, was, were, be, being, been, will be, can be, might be, has been, have been, had been, would have been, might have been, etc.). Other linking verbs that are often used include: *seem, appear, look, become, grow, taste, feel, smell, sound, remain,* and *stay*. Verb phrases include the main verb and are preceded by a helping verb. When a helping verb is added, the main verb may change its form. The most common helping verbs are the "be" verbs (e.g., has, have, had, shall, will, can, may, should, would, could, might, must, do did, and does).

Adverbs are words used to define or modify verbs, adjectives, or other adverbs, and they answer: Where?; when?; how?, and to what extent? Adverbs are also used in sentences that are questions.

A preposition is a word showing the relationship of a noun (or pronoun) to another word in a sentence. Common prepositions include: *About, above, across, after, against, along, amid, among, around, at, before, behind, below, beneath, beside, between, beyond, but, by, down, during, except, for, from, in, into, like, near, of, off, on, over, past, since, through, throughout, to, toward, under, underneath, until, up, upon, with, within,* and *without*. Compound prepositions also show the relationship of a noun to another word in a sentence and appear in the form of a two or three word phrase (e.g., according to, because of, instead of, in spite of, on account of, out of).

Conjunctions are joining words used to join clauses and sentences. There are three general types of conjunctions. Coordinating conjunctions include: *and, but, for* (when used to connect sentences), *nor, or,* and *yet*. Correlative conjunctions are used in pairs (e.g., either...or; neither...nor; both...and; and not only...but also). Subordinating conjunctions are used to introduce an adverb clause (e.g., since, if).

An interjection is a word used to express emotion, often stands alone, and is usually followed by an exclamation point (e.g., Oh!; and Wow!). Interjections are commonly found in dialogue. Table 11.4 shows the parts of speech and could be displayed in a classroom writing center as a reminder. The chart could be adapted for different age levels.

Another related area for instructional focus in the parts of speech includes the use of phrases and clauses. For example, a phrase is a group of related words (not containing a verb and its subject) used to modify another word in a sentence. That is, the phrase is used as a single part of speech. There are verb phrases, prepositional phrases, and participial phrases. Prepositional phrases begin with a preposition and end with a noun (or pronoun). An adjective phrase is a prepositional phrase used to define a noun or pronoun and usually follows the word it modifies. An adverb phrase is a prepositional phrase that is often used to define a verb, and it is sometimes used to modify an adjective or adverb. An adverb phrase may be separated from the word it modifies. A participial phrase is a group of related words that contains a participle and acts as an adjective in a sentence. As a point of clarification, a participle is a word formed from a verb and is used as an adjective. Present participles end in *ing*, and past participles end in *ed, d*, and, *t*.

Table 11.4. The Parts of Speech

Noun: A word that is used to name a person, place, thing, or idea
Pronoun: A word that stands for a noun
Adjective: A word that describes or defines a noun or pronoun
Verb: Action Verb: A word used to express action (physical or mental) Linking Verb: Links its subject with a noun or adjective in the predicate
Adverb: A word used to define or modify a verb, adjective, or another adverb
Preposition: A word showing the relationship of noun (or pronoun) to another word in a sentence
Conjunction: A joining word
Interjection: A word used to express emotion (often a word which stands alone and is followed by an exclamation point)

The term clause is used to refer to a group of words containing a verb and its subject. The independent clause can stand alone as a complete sentence, because it expresses a complete thought. On the other hand, a subordinate clause cannot stand alone as a complete sentence, because it does not express a complete thought. Subordinate clauses contain verbs and their subjects and are introduced by words such as *since, when, if, as, who, which,* and *that*. These words prevent the clauses from standing alone.

An adjective clause is a subordinate clause that is used as an adjective to define a noun (or pronoun). Adjective clauses are usually introduced by a relative pronoun (who, who, whose, which, that). Sometimes the relative pronoun is preceded by a preposition, in order to avoid ending a clause or sentence with a preposition. Adjective clauses usually follow immediately after the words they modify

An adverb clause is a subordinate clause that is used as an adverb to modify a verb, adjective, or adverb. Adverb clauses generally define how, when, where, why, to what extent, and under what conditions, and when an adverb clause occurs at the beginning of a sentence, it is usually followed by a comma. In addition, adverb clauses are usually introduced by a subordinating conjunction (e.g., after, although, as, as if, as long as, as soon as, because, before, if, in order that, since, so that, than, though, unless, until, when, whenever, where, wherever, and while).

A complete sentence is a complete thought. That is, it has a subject, a verb, and a complement (when needed to complete the meaning). A complement is the term used to refer to a word that completes the meaning introduced by the subject and verb. A complement often answers the what, or who question. A direct object is a word that receives the action of the verb, or names the result of the action of the verb (directly), follows the action verb, and answers what, or whom. On the other hand, an indirect object identifies to what, to whom, for what, for whom the action of the verb is directed. In general, sentences have both an indirect and a direct object.

The term subject complement is used to refer to a word following a linking verb that explains or describes the subject. Predicate nominatives are nouns and pronouns in the predicate which refer to the subject, while predicate adjectives are adjectives in the predicate which modify the subject.

There are several sentence structure types that teachers should model, explicitly teach, and provide children with many opportunities for practice within authentic writing tasks. The sentence structure types include simple, compound, complex, and compound-complex as illustrated in Figure 11.3.

Simple sentences contain a word or a group of words that express a complete thought. That is, a simple sentence can stand alone with no other clauses attached to it. Although a simple sentence has only one independent clause and no subordinate clauses, it may have a compound subject or a compound verb.

On the other hand, a compound sentence has two or more independent clauses that are joined by conjunctions (e.g., and, but, or, nor, for). However, the compound sentence does not have any subordinate clauses.

Alternatively, the complex sentence contains one independent clause and one or more subordinate clauses, and the compound-complex sentence has two or more independent clauses and one or more subordinate clauses. Using a variety of sentence structure types provides variety and interest in written expression. Children should be encouraged to use a variety of sentence structures in both their speaking and writing. Examples of the various types of sentences can be posted in a classroom, in a writing center, or on prompt cards as visual reminders for young writers.

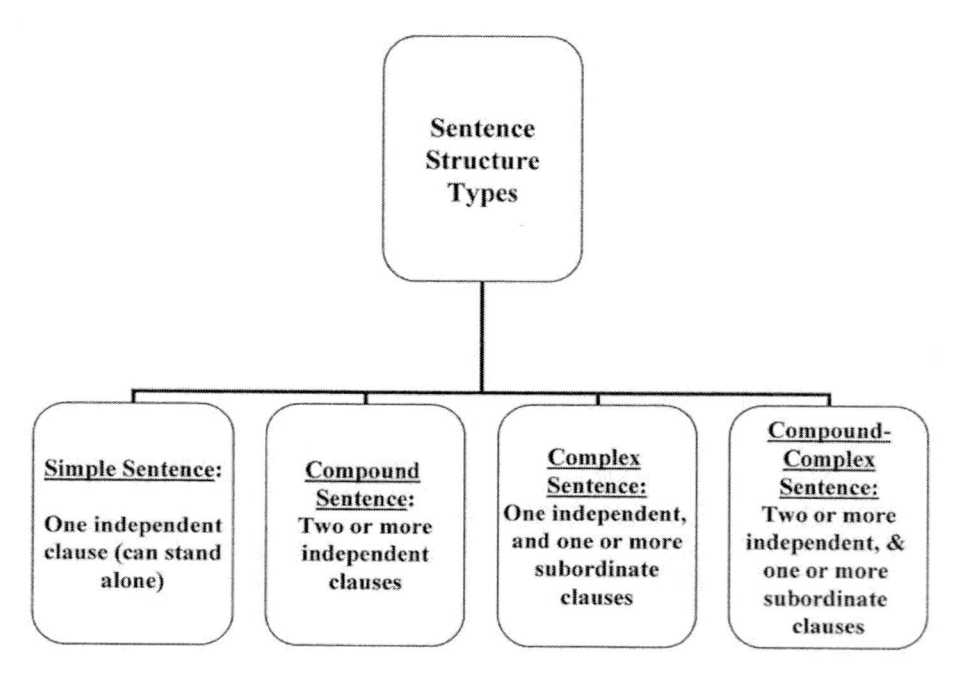

Figure 11.3. Sentence Structure Types.

GENERAL GUIDELINES FOR WRITTEN EXPRESSION ASSIGNMENTS

As children advance, they should have many experiences with different types of writing. Once children are responsible for writing formal papers, such as reports or essays and compositions, they need guidance in some general standards. First, they need to know that it is important to follow each teacher's specific instructions for any writing project. Then they can be given some general instructions for the format of written work (with a prompt card at first) as illustrated in Table 11.5.

Table 11.5. General Instructions for Paper Writing

Use standard size paper (8.5 X 11 inches)
Use black or blue ink (for handwritten); black ink for computer printouts of written work
Use 1-inch margins; double-spaced if typed
Indent first line of each paragraph
Include identifying information—name, date, etc., with the paper (often on the top of first page)
Title (if there is one) is centered on the first line of the paper; then skip a line to begin the paper
Beginning with page 2, include page numbers on each page
Acceptable common abbreviations: Mr., Mrs., Dr., Jr., Sr., P.M., A.M.
Numbers: Always spell out a number that begins a sentence
All handwritten work should be neat and legible
Numbers of more than two words are written in numerals (120 children
Write out numbers like first, second, and third

MECHANICS REVIEW

Capitalization

The mechanics of writing include capitalization, punctuation, and to some extent, spelling. Spelling is also covered in the discussion of morphology and language in other chapters. Capitalization is used to indicate important words such as those that occur at the beginning of sentences, proper nouns, and titles.

The use of capital letters in writing one's own name is one of the first capitalization rules young writers learn. There are many other capitalization rules that need to be a part of the teaching/learning cylce as children develop their abilities as writers. Some important initial capitalization rules include the following: Capitalize the first word in sentences; the pronoun I; and proper nouns, as in the names of persons, streets, towns, bodies of water, islands, parks, mountains, government bodies, institutions, businesses and organizations, states, countries, and continents. Exceptions include the following: Do not capitalize north, south, east, and west when they refer to a direction; or school, restaurant, and club, unless they are part of a proper name. As children gain more experience with reading and writing, they should learn additional capitalization rules such as:

Capitalize the names of special events, calendar related items, historical events and periods, nationalities, races, religions, brand names, ships, planets, awards, and monuments; capitalize proper adjectives formed from proper nouns (e.g., China, Chinese); capitalize the title of a person when it comes before a name, a title showing family relationship when used with a person's name (e.g., Uncle Steve), and a title showing family relationship in place of a person's name (e.g., Ask Grandma.). When children begin to give titles to their written work or write titles of books in their book reports, they learn to capitalize all important words (including first word and last word) in titles of books, newspapers, poems, songs, stories, movies, paintings, and other pieces. In addition, they learn that it is correct to capitalize words which refer to the Deity (God, Lord, the Creator, Son of God), while the word god is not capitalized when referring to pagan deities (sun god).

Punctuation

Punctuation is an important and sometimes undervalued system. Marks of punctuation allow the writer to convey meaning clearly to the reader. Just as the speaker uses voice, intonation, rhythm, volume, emphasis, and pausing to convey meaning, so does the writer with the use of marks of punctuation. Understanding the system of punctuation will enable children to read more fluently and write more clearly.

End marks include the punctuation marks at the end of a sentence or an abbreviation. The punctuation at the end of a sentence indicates a full stop. Statements are followed by periods; questions are followed by question marks; exclamations are followed by exclamation points; and imperative sentences may be followed by either periods or exclamation points. Although abbreviations are also followed by periods, they do not indicate a full stop.

Similarly, a comma is used to signal the reader. However, a comma divides a sentence into readable parts by indicating pauses to the reader rather than full stops. Therefore, commas are used to separate words in a series; before the *and* which joins the last two items in a series to make the meaning clear; to separate phrases in a series; to separate subordinate clauses and short independent clauses in a series. However, when all items in a series are joined by the word *and* or the word *or*, commas do not need to separate them. In addition, commas are used to separate two or more adjectives preceding a noun, except when the last adjective before a noun is so closely connected to the noun that they seem to form one expression (e.g., The young girl relied on her small, tough, fearless dog.); before the words *and, but, or, nor, for,* and *yet* when they join independent clauses; to set off participial phrases or adjective clauses when they are not essential to the meaning of a sentence; after a participial phrase or adverb clause that begins a sentence (e.g., Forced out of the competition by her injury, Amanda was determined to recover quickly.); to set off an interrupter (of course, well, a person's name, an appositive—a word or phrase that means the same thing as the noun it follows); after the following words when they begin a sentence (yes, no, well,); to set off words used in direct address (e.g., Jennie, would you rather go to Santa Monica or Santa Barbara?); to set off parenthetical expressions (e.g., in fact, however, for example, of course, for instance, on the contrary, nevertheless, I believe, to tell the truth, in my opinion, mind you, as I was saying); and to separate items in dates and addresses.

The semicolon is used to signal a pause greater than a comma but not as great as a period. For example a semicolon may be used between any independent clauses in a sentence when they are not joined by *and, but, or, nor, for, yet*; between independent clauses joined by the following: *for example, for instance, moreover, that is, furthermore, otherwise, therefore, however, consequently, instead, hence, besides, accordingly*; or to separate independent clauses of a compound sentence if there are commas within the clauses.

The colon is the mark of punctuation which indicates that something will follow. For example a colon should be used before a list of items—especially after the phrases *as follows* or *the following*. In addition, colons are used between the hour and minute in expression of time, as well as after the salutation of a business letter.

Since most children have enjoyable experiences with read-alouds, one of the first types of writing they are excited to try is story-writing, and they are likely to want to try to include some dialogue in their stories. Therefore, they need some guidance in the use of quotation marks. Quotation marks signal the reader that a person's exact words appear within the quotation marks. There are some initial concepts that will help children as both readers and writers. For example, when writing dialogue, begin a new paragraph each time the speakers change. This helps the reader keep track of who is speaking. Some general guidelines for punctuation within dialogue include the following: In dialogue when a sentence is divided into two parts by an interrupting expression such as she said, the second part begins with a lower case letter (unless the word is a proper noun); within a sentence a direct quote is set off from the rest of the sentence with a comma, question mark, or exclamation point inside the quotation marks (e.g., "What a wonderful view!" exclaimed Erin.); periods or commas which follow a quotation are placed inside the closing quotation marks; when a quotation contains more than one sentence, use quotations marks only at the beginning and end of the entire quotation; and single quotation marks are used to enclose a quote within a quote.

Another type of punctuation that helps readers is the apostrophe. The apostrophe is used to show ownership or a relationship, and where letters were omitted in a contraction. See Tables 11.6 for examples.

Table 11.6. Apostrophe Use

Possessive of singular noun—add an apostrophe and an s
Possessive of plural noun ending in s—add only the apostrophe
If a proper name ends in s (and has two or more syllables) add only the apostrophe
An apostrophe takes the place of the omitted letters in a contraction When not is added to a verb it is often contracted (e.g., is not, isn't; are not, aren't; does not, doesn't; do not, don't) When a double consonant occurs, the spelling changes (e.g., will not, won't; cannot, can't)
Nouns or pronouns and verbs may form contractions (I am, I'm; you are, you're; they are, they're; Carol is, Carol's)
Use an apostrophe and an s to form the plural of letters, numbers, and signs: She learned all her ABC's. He makes his 7's look like 1's. You may use &'s on the sign.
Word Differences: Apostrophe Use Its and it's: Its is a possessive pronoun and has no apostrophe It's may be a contraction of it is or it has Whose and who's: Whose is a possessive pronoun (e.g., Whose idea was it anyway?) Who's is a contraction meaning who is or who has Your and You're: Your is a possessive pronoun (e.g., Your writing has improved.) You're is a contraction of you are

The final mark of punctuation to be discussed here is the hyphen. In handwritten work, a hyphen is used to divide a word between syllables at the end of a line when not enough space remains for the entire word. In addition, hyphens are used to write some compound words, such as the compound numbers twenty-one through ninety-nine, and fractions used as adjectives (e.g., A two-thirds majority).

WRITING AND TEXT STRUCTURE

Text Structure at the Sentence Level

As presented previously in this chapter, the writer signals the reader through the use of punctuation marks. For example, a writer signals the end of sentences with end marks so that the reader knows to pause, and that they have reached the end of a complete thought. When a sentence does not contain a complete thought, it is referred to as a sentence fragment. That is, a fragment is a sentence part that cannot stand alone. Sentence fragments are a common problem and should be addressed through teacher modeling, explicit instruction, practice and application. Another frequent problem at the sentence level is the run-on sentence. A run-on sentence contains two or more sentences with either no punctuation or only commas. Therefore, the following sentence level concepts should be included in writing instruction (See Table 11.7).

Table 11.7. Text Structure at the Sentence Level

Complete Sentence:
A sentence has both a verb and subject
A sentence expresses a complete thought
Complete sentence: One of their favorite things is reading bedtime stories every night.
Complete sentence: We went shopping in Saratoga, a picturesque town near Albany.
Fragments
A subordinate clause is not a complete sentence
Example: As the writer continued. (Although this example has a subject and verb, it does not express a complete thought. The reader is left wondering what happened.)
Relative pronouns (who, whom, whose, which, that) and subordinating conjunctions (after, although, as, because, before, if, in order, since, so that, than, though, unless, until, when, whenever, where, wherever, while) introduce subordinate clauses.
A verb phrase is not a complete sentence
Example: Reading bedtime stories every night.
An appositive phrase is not a complete sentence
Example: A picturesque town near Albany.
An appositive phrase defines the noun or pronoun it follows
Run-on sentences: Two or more sentences with no punctuation or only a comma.
A comma marks a pause or break in a sentence, not the end
Example: May I borrow your book, I'll give it back tomorrow.
Corrected: May I borrow your book? I'll give it back tomorrow.

One of the important elements of sentence writing is variety. This is an element of writing style. That is, writing is more interesting when attention is given to the flow of the writing. Groups of sentences that are choppy or abrupt, with no variety in construction, or sentences that ramble due to a string of conjunctions, should be avoided.

The following suggestions may prove helpful in generating sentence variety and interest. First, help children construct compound sentences with sentence combining practice. Teach them to combine two short related sentences using a conjunction (e.g., *and, but, or, nor*) and a comma to join the two closely related independent clauses. Another way to create interest is to combine short, choppy sentences, using subordinate clauses to construct complex sentences. Another suggestion for creating interest is to vary how sentences begin. In other words, begin some sentences with the subject, some with a modifier, some with an adverb or adverb clause, and some with a prepositional phrase. Finally, teach children to avoid creating rambling sentences. Rambling sentences are those which use several or more conjunctions. It is better to break sentences into clauses and combine some clauses into compound or complex sentences. Furthermore, reading passages aloud may help children determine whether or not a selection flows and if there is enough variety in the types of sentences used.

Text Structure at the Paragraph Level

A paragraph is a subdivision of a written composition that consists of one or more sentences dealing with one topic, and each new paragraph begins on a new indented line (Merriam Webster's Collegiate Dictionary, 1997). Paragraphs help the reader comprehend the organization of the piece of writing. For example, a new paragraph is a cue to the reader that the author is moving to another idea. Generally, the topic of a paragraph is stated in a topic sentence, and the rest of the paragraph consists of sentences that develop that main idea or topic through the use of supporting details. The topic sentence is often the first sentence in a paragraph. It is often helpful to imagine the sandwich approach to writing a paragraph. Visualize what a sandwich looks like. The first layer (the top piece of bread) tells the reader what the paragraph is going to be about. The middle layers (the filling of the sandwich) give the reader the supporting details and develop the topic sentence. Finally, when a paragraph is long or complicated, the last layer (the bottom piece of bread) is used to summarize the topic or restate the main point of the paragraph. This is known as the concluding sentence and is used as needed. The sandwich approach is a very visual way to illustrate how to write a cohesive paragraph.

A cohesive paragraph is one in which all the sentences develop, explain, or support the topic sentence or main idea. When sentences deviate from this support, the paragraph loses its wholeness and the reader may be confused. Cohesiveness is one of the essential qualities of written expression.

Another essential quality is coherence. This has to do with the organization and logical order of sentences. When sentences are arranged in a logical sequence, comprehension is enhanced for the reader. The writer should plan the arrangement of sentences. Depending on the type of writing, the sequence of sentences may be determined by time or chronological order, the order of steps in a process, spatial position, or the order of importance. The goal is to have a logical or natural flow to sentence order in a paragraph. Oftentimes, transitional expressions are used to help clarify the relation of one sentence to another. The following transitional words may be used to indicate a chronological relationship: *after, finally, first, later, meanwhile, next, now, soon,* and *then.* In addition, the following transitional expressions may be used to indicate a spatial relationship: *above, ahead, behind, beyond, inside, near,* and *outside.* Furthermore, the following transitional expressions are often used to show a relationship between ideas: *consequently, in addition, in conclusion, as a result, furthermore, in fact, however, moreover, similarly, therefore, on the other hand,* and *on the contrary.* All of these transitional expressions help the reader better understand the relationship between sentences and the organization of the ideas in a paragraph.

Planning is essential to the writing process. The first step in planning a paragraph is to think about the topic. The second step is to write the topic sentence. With the topic sentence in mind, it is helpful to make a list of supporting ideas. This list can then be used to write sentences that support and develop the topic in a clear and cohesive manner. While the topic sentence is a general statement, the supporting details are more specific sentences and include examples, facts, and reasons. A good rule of thumb is to include at least two supporting detail sentences when developing a paragraph.

One way to develop a paragraph is to include the retelling of an incident. Just as the previous example, the first two steps are to think about the topic and write the topic sentence. Then, instead of using a series of supporting facts or details, an anecdote is used to support the topic sentence.

Another way to develop a paragraph is to support an opinion through the use of reasons why or why not. Giving the reader the reasons why or why not is done in an effort to persuade the reader that an opinion is correct. This type of paragraph begins with the topic sentence or opinion and is followed by a series of reasons that support the opinion.

In conclusion, children need to see models of expert writing, explicit instruction, and many opportunities to practice using standard writing conventions within the context of real writing activities. They need to learn how to convey their intended message clearly so that the reader is able to receive it. They need practice and support choosing words and using words in their writing, as well as practice using correct forms of grammar (e.g., parts of speech, verb-subject agreement, modifiers, and text structure elements). In addition, children need to know how to use resources, such as a dictionary, to help them become independent learners. Finally, children need to be able to use the elements of grammar, punctuation, capitalization, word use, and spelling efficiently so that they are able to communicate effectively with their intended audience. However, writing conventions are only part of the equation of written expression. The other part is the writing process.

QUESTIONS FOR REFLECTION AND DISCUSSION

1) How will you make learning about grammar in written expression interesting for your students?
2) How can writing convention instruction be incorporated into a comprehensive writing program?

CHAPTER APPLICATION EXERCISES

1) Write a short story about a special childhood memory. Assume your audience is a group of first grade children. Plan your story before you write. Then as you write, try to use the suggestions from the chapter to make your piece interesting. Try to use interesting and precise adjectives and adverbs, and a variety of sentence structures. Be sure to keep your audience in mind.
2) Interview a primary level teacher about how he or she teaches the elements of writing. Write a short one-page report. Use the suggestions in the chapter to write an exemplary paper.

Chapter 12

THE WRITING PROCESS

"[Writing is] a little like a quiet explosion in your head."
(Maurice Sendak, children's book author)

The elements of grammar, punctuation, capitalization, word use, spelling, and sentence structure are critically important components of writing, but they are only part of the story of writing. The other part of the story is often referred to as the writing process. The writing process can be thought of as the act of getting ideas across in a written format. This process is vital so that authors communicate effectively with their audiences. Planning, organization, use of vocabulary, main ideas, and supporting details all contribute to effective written expression. This is true whether the writing is narrative, expository, or persuasive.

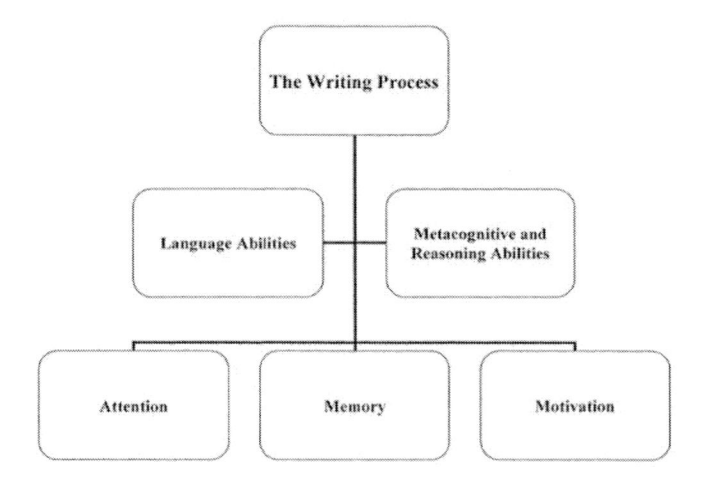

Figure 12.1. The Complex Nature of the Writing Process.

The process of writing is not an easy course of action. Writing is a complex and later developing language skill. In fact, Moats (1991, p. 190) suggests that writing, "may be impaired by dysfunction in any of the psychological processes required to write well." Figure 12.1 illustrates the complex nature of the writing process.

EXPOSITORY WRITING

Expository writing is informational writing. The writer presents information about a subject. The objective of expository writing is to help the reader understand something or learn something. Both textbooks and reports are examples of expository writing. As children progress through the grade levels in school, more and more learning is dependent on the comprehension and production of expository writing. They are required to link writing and reading. Figure 12.2 illustrates the overlap and mutual influence of several factors in the expository writing process. Children need to know that writing is indeed a process—that writers do not simply sit down with pen in hand (or at a keyboard) and produce a final product in one sitting. Teachers should model each phase of the writing process so that children can "see" how writers write.

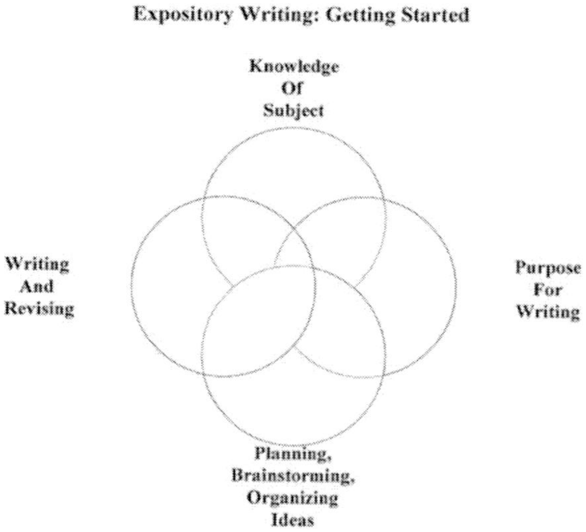

Figure 12.2. Expository Writing: Getting Started.

When teaching children to compose a piece of expository writing, it is important to explicitly teach the steps of the writing process, and research supports this as a way to positively influence the quality of children's writing (Baker, Gersten, & Graham, 2003).

Children should be knowledgeable about the subject they are going to write about. Children gain knowledge (build background) in a variety of ways—through experiences, both personal and vicarious, and through reading and listening. Together these experiences contribute to their knowledge about a writing subject. In addition to the selection of a topic, teachers should help children keep the specific purpose for writing in mind (i.e., to inform, persuade, etc.). Along with the purpose, children need to be supported in learning how to write with an audience in mind.

The next phase of the expository writing process is planning. First, teachers should model and then provide practice so that children are able to brainstorm ideas about a topic, list ideas, review and remove ideas, group closely related ideas, create headings, and finally create a tentative outline. The outline may be in the form of a graphic organizer which may help organize the writing in a clear and logical way. For example, ideas could be sequenced by time, arranged from general to specific, or arranged by their importance.

The graphic organizer may be set up to illustrate the three basic components of an expository composition (i.e., the introduction, body, and conclusion). Figure 12.3 shows an example of a basic graphic organizer. After initial instruction, children's learning may be scaffolded with think sheets or cue cards that they keep with them while writing.

As children advance through elementary school and continue to develop their expository writing skills, they should be taught to connect ideas and paragraphs with transitional expressions in order to help the flow of the writing and make smooth connections. Some examples include: *first, then, next, in addition, even more, furthermore, moreover, therefore, nevertheless, on the other hand, besides, thus, for example, in fact,* and *finally.*

Teachers should model and then scaffold learning as children move through the process of revising their writing. When children read their own writing, it is often helpful to have them read the composition aloud and ask the following questions: Does it make sense?; and Does it flow? Then, any confusing sentences or paragraphs can be targeted for revision. In the process, any unnecessary or confusing words or phrases can be eliminated or changed, punctuation can be checked (i.e., does the punctuation help the reader understand?), and spelling can be reviewed for accuracy.

Informational Writing

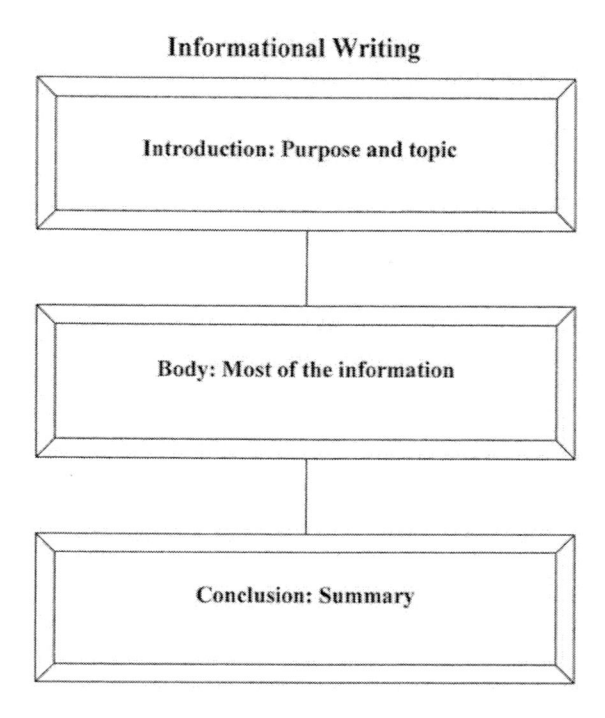

Figure 12.3. Graphic Organizer: Expository Composition.

Specific kinds of expository writing should be included in writing instruction. For example, summarization (i.e., writing in one's own words the main ideas of another's writing) instruction should include the following guidelines: A summary should be no longer than a third of the original piece; a summary should include the main ideas (but restated in the child's own words); and the original writing source—the basis for the summary—should be acknowledged.

Another kind of expository writing that should be included in instruction is the report. Report writing deserves specific attention and requires the coordination of many components. Reports require that children gather and organize information from several or more sources. To help organize the various parameters of this large writing task, children can learn to use self-questioning strategies. For example, children may be guided to think about the following: What is the purpose of the report?; What are the requirements of the report (e.g., topic, length, due date, etc.)?; What are the steps (i.e., gathering and reading information; organizing information; writing and revising the report), and within each step, What are the sub-steps? For example in gathering information, children need to know how to locate sources, and how to determine reliable sources from questionable sources. Then they need to know how to read, highlight, take notes and record sources of information. Next children should learn how to organize notes according to idea categories and headings and create an outline based on notes. Report writing is a complex task. Therefore, children may need concrete reminders of the critical steps as illustrated in Figure 12.4. This will scaffold the task as they gain experience and develop their skills.

Writing and Revising a Report

Write Report (Based on notes and outline)		Revise Report: Read report (aloud to listen to how it sounds)
Follow basic form: Introduction, body, conclusion	Content: Accuracy, Completeness	
Try to capture reader's attention at the beginning	Style: Is it interesting? Does it grab attention?	
Use variety of sentence structure and vocabulary	Construction: All parts included? Variety?	
Pay attention to the flow of the report	Form: Does it flow? Follow rubric?	

Figure 12.4. Report Writing Graphic Organizer.

Explicit instruction in how to write and revise a report may begin with teacher modeling using a think-aloud, followed by interactive writing as a group and followed by supported writing during practice. Here are some of the essential considerations to teach about report writing. First, the first draft is based on notes and the outline. The basic form includes an introduction, the body, and a conclusion. Children need guidance and practice in using a variety of sentence structure and vocabulary in their writing. As writers, children should keep their intended reader in mind as they try to capture the reader's attention at the beginning of the report. In addition, they should give attention to the flow of the report. Self-questioning techniques that ask the following may be helpful: Are the details in a logical sequence?; Does the report make sense?; and Did I use transition words (e.g., *first, next, later*) within and between paragraph? In preparation for revising the report, it is often helpful (particularly for students with learning disabilities) to have students read the report aloud. Then the report can be revised according to the following elements: The content, which includes both accuracy and thoroughness; the construction and style, which includes the main parts of a report (i.e., introduction, body with supporting details, and conclusion), interesting ideas, and well-constructed sentences and paragraphs; and form, which includes the expectations and requirements for the format (e.g., identifying information, title, sources, etc.).

NARRATIVE WRITING

A narrative is a story. Storytellers in the oral tradition create interesting, humorous, thrilling, and emotional stories through their use of language, tone of voice, volume, use of gestures and facial expressions. Story writers, those who write narratives, do the same thing with the written word. Similar to other kinds of writing, narrative writing requires planning and knowledge. In addition, most narratives follow a form called a story grammar.

Through mini-lessons, teachers can model and explain various writing skills and strategies. Children should then be provided with an opportunity to practice (with guidance). Figure 12.5 illustrates a writing prompt card that gives children some concrete guidance for story planning.

After children gain experience and skill with planning, they can then proceed to write a first draft. At this point, the teacher should use a think-aloud to model and explain how he or she writes a first draft. Interactive or shared writing can be used to reinforce the newly introduced concepts, and children can help create think sheets to use later as they practice writing narratives with teacher and peer support.

As children advance in their writing skills throughout elementary school, they begin to develop narrative writing skills which include the following qualities: The ability to include specific details to make the action come alive (i.e., show the reader what happened through the use of details); the ability to make use of specific verbs that help the reader form a clear image of the action (e.g., using *strut* instead of *walk*); using dialogue to make the story livelier, more realistic, and allow the reader to get to know the personality of the characters; and the ability to accurately use quotation marks to identify who is talking. In addition, the following qualities are held in high regard for narrative writers: The ability to use vivid and convincing descriptions such that the reader sees, hears, tastes, and otherwise experiences something; the ability to use descriptions to bring characters and settings alive; the ability to make comparisons to describe people or events; and the ability to transport the reader in time and space.

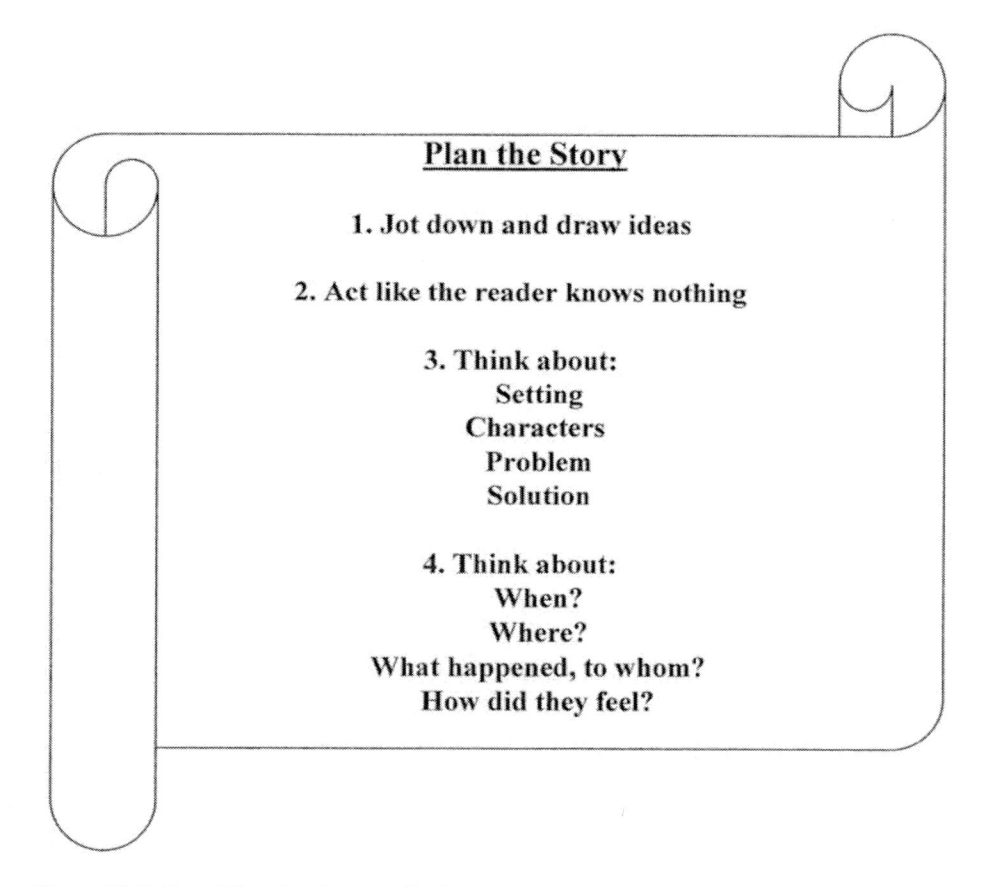

Figure 12.5. Story Planning Prompt Card.

When the first draft of a story is finished, children should be encouraged to read the draft aloud. This allows the child and others if they are working in a writing group, to hear the story. The revision process follows the guidelines for other kinds of writing. First, the writer asks and answers questions such as: Does the story make sense? Does it flow? Then any details that do not support the story or any confusing dialogue or descriptions are changed to make the story better.

Finding Balance

In reviewing all the elements and skills involved in writing it is important to realize that there has to be a balance between emphasis on the pure ideas and the form in which those ideas are communicated. In written expression there is a marriage of form and function. The ideas are what initiates and propels any piece of writing onward, and the structure of the piece (everything from spelling to punctuation to paragraph structure) determines how well the thoughts and ideas are delivered. When form and function combine effectively, the reader is then able to fully participate in a glorious interaction between the writer's intentions and what the reader brings to the process.

That being said, it is important to focus on both encouraging children to explore themselves and their worlds, while at the same time encouraging them to present their ideas in the best possible way so that they are fully understood. This is an ever-evolving process, and children need many opportunities to practice and develop their writing skills. Children need to learn that writing is indeed a process, just as thinking is an on-going process in which we rethink things and often revise our opinions based on new information. That is to say, there is always room for revising, making things better, tweaking. When we teach children that growth and development involves looking at things in new ways, we give them the opportunity to try without fear of failure. We need to teach children that academic skills are just like any other skills that we learn as human beings. We are not experts right away. For example, when young children learn to walk, it takes practice and many episodes of not getting it quite right before they are able to toddle their way across a room, let alone run across the yard. The same is true of writing skills. Many episodes of not getting it quite right happen along the journey of becoming writers. It is not necessary to create a masterpiece every time, but it is necessary to do a great deal of writing to hone skills and experiment with ideas. This is how children learn how to write.

In conclusion, opportunities to write should be integrated as part of a child's learning process such that writing tasks are not viewed as unusual events that are always subject to assessment. In this process, ideas are honored, and hopefully the child's voice will be heard. The goal of writing instruction should be to find a balance between the ideas contained in children's writing and how children learn to best communicate those ideas to their readers.

QUESTIONS FOR REFLECTION AND DISCUSSION

1) Writing may be viewed as involving both a product and a process. Think about how you learned to write as a child. What was the focus? Describe your earliest memories of writing.
2) How did your early experiences with writing influence your self-efficacy as a writer?
3) How will you help the children you teach to become confident and proficient writers?

CHAPTER APPLICATION EXERCISES

1) Observe a primary classroom as they work on writing in their literacy block. How are the children engaged in prewriting, composing, revising, editing, and publishing? What strategies do they find useful?
2) Write a one-page report of your findings. As you write, reflect on the strategies you use to help you in your writing process. What are your strengths? What do you need to work on? How will you remedy any areas that need work?

REFERENCES

Adams, J. (1794). *Letter to Abigal Adams, December 28, 1794.* Adams papers, Massachusetts Historical Society, Boston.

Algozzine, B., Marr, M.B., Kavel, R., & Dugan, K.K. (2009). Using peer coaches to build oral reading fluency. *Journal of Education for Students Placed at Risk, 14*, 256-270.

Andersen, H.C. (1861). *The snow man.* New Fairy Tales and Stories, (Second Series, First Collection). Copenhagen, Denmark: C.A. Reitzel

Anderson, R.C., & Nagy, W.E. (1993). *The vocabulary conundrum. Technical Report No. 570.* Center for the Study of Reading, Urbana, IL. Office of Educational Research and Improvement, Washington. DC.

Archambault, I., Eccles, J.S., & Vida, M.N. (2010). Ability self-concepts and subjective value in literacy: Joint trajectories from grades 1 through 12. *Journal of Educational Psychology, 102*(4), 804-816.

Bacon, F. (1561-1626). From religious meditations. In L.D. Eigen, & J.P. Siegel (Eds.)(1993), *The Macmillian dictionary of politial quotations*, 1993. New York: Macmillian Publishing Company.

Baker, S., Gersten, R., & Graham, S. (2003). Teaching expressive writing to students with learning disabilities: Research-based applications and examples. *Journal of Learning Disabilities, 36*, 109-123.

Bateman, B.D. (2007). Law and the conceptual foundations of special education practice. In J.B. Crockett, M.M. Gerber, & T.J. Landrum (Eds.), *Achieving the radical reform of special education: Essays in honor of James M. Kauffman* (pp. 95-114). Mahwah, NJ: Lawrence Erlbaum Associates.

Becker, M., McElvany, N., & Kortenbruck, M. (2010). Intrinsic and extrinsic reading motivation as predictors of reading literacy: A longitudinal study. *Journal of Educational Psychology, 102*(4), 773-785.

Boulware-Gooden, R., Carreker, S., Thornhill, A., & Joshi, R. (2007). Instruction of metacognitive strategies enhances reading comprehension and vocabulary achievement of third grade students. *The Reading Teacher, 61*, 70-77.

Campbell, J. (1988). *The power of myth.* New York: Doubleday.

Carnine, D.W., Silbert, J., Kame'enui, E.J., & Tarver, S. (2010). *Direct reading instruction.* Boston, MA: Pearson Education, Inc.

Catts, H.W, & Kamhi, A.G. (2005). *Language and reading disabilities.* Boston, MA: Allyn and Bacon.

Chard, D.J., Vaughn, S., & Tyler, B. (2002). A synthesis of research on effective interventions for building reading fluency with elementary students with learning disabilities. *Journal of Learning Disabilities, 35*, 386—406.

Chomsky, N. (1965). *Aspects of the theory of syntax.* Cambridge, MA: MIT Press.

Cicero, M.T. (106 BC – 43 BC). Roman author. In S. Platt (Ed.)(1997), *Respectfully quoted: A dictionary of quotations*, 1997. New York: Barnes and Noble.

Ebbers, S.M., & Denton, C.A. (2008). A root awakening: Vocabulary instruction for older students with reading difficulties. *Learning Disabilities Research and Practice, 23*, 90-102.

Faggella-Luby, M.N., & Deshler, D.D. (2008). Reading comprehension in adolescents with LD: What we know; what we need to learn. *Learning Disabilities Research and Practice 23*(2), 70-78.

Ferguson, D.L. (2008). International trends in inclusive education: The continuing challenge to teach each and everyone. *European Journal of Special Needs Education, 23*(2), 109-120.

Ferrara, S.L. (2005). Reading fluency and self-efficacy: A case study. *International Journal of Disability, Development and Education, 52*(3), 215-231.

Ferrara, W., Dougherty, F., & Boer, G. (1991). *Managerial cost accounting: Planning and control.* Houston, TX: Dame Publications, Inc.

Fraser, J., & Conti-Ramsden, G. (2008). Contribution of phonological and broader language skills to literacy. *International Journal of Language and Communication Disorders, 43*(5), 552-569.

Fuchs, D., Fuchs, L., & Stecker (2010*).* The blurring of special education in a new continuum of general education placements and services. *Exceptional Children, 76*(3), 301-323.

Gambrell, L. (1996). Creating classroom cultures that foster motivation. *The Reading Teacher, 50*, 14-25.

Gagne, R.M., & Dirscoll, M.P. (1988). *Essentials of learning for instruction.* Englewood Cliffs, NJ: Prentice Hall.

Geisel, T. (1963). *Hop on Pop, by Dr. Seuss.* New York, NY: Random House.

Gersten, R., Fuchs, L., Williams, J., & Baker, S. (2001). Teaching reading comprehension strategies to students with learning disabilities: A review of research. *Review of Educational Research, 71*, 279-320.

Gillam, R.G., & Bedore, L.M. (2000). Communication across the lifespan. In R.B. Gillam, T.P., Marquardt, & F.N. Marin, (Eds.), *Communication sciences and disorders: From science to clinical practice* (pp. 25-61). San Diego, CA: Singular Publishing.

Gladwell, M. (2008). *Outliers: The story of success.* New York, NY: Little, Brown and Company.

Goodwin, A.P. & Ahn, S. (2010). A meta-analysis of morphological interventions: Effects on literacy achievement of children with literacy difficulties. *Annals of Dyslexia, 60*, 183–208.

Gunning, T.G. (2010). *Creating literacy instruction for all students* (7th Ed.). Boston, MA: Pearson Education, Inc.

Hallahan, D.P., Kauffman, J.M., & Pullen, P. (2010). *Exceptional learners* (11th ed.). Boston, MA: Allyn and Bacon.

Hallahan, D.P., Loyd, J.W., Kauffman, J.M., Weiss, M.P., & Martinez, E.A. (2005). *Learning disabilities: Foundations, characteristics, and effective teaching.* Boston, MA: Allyn and Bacon.

Harris, A.J., & Sipay, E.R. (1990). *How to increase reading ability.* New York: Longman.

Heckleman, R.G. (1969). A neurological-impress method of remedial-reading instruction. *Academic Therapy, 4*, 277-282.

Holmes, O.W. (1918). *Town v. Eisner,* 245 U.S. 425.

Hoover, J.J., & Patton, J.R. (2008). The role of special educators in a multi-tiered Instructional system. *Intervention in School and Clinic, 43*(4), 195-202.

Individuals with Disabilities Education Improvement Act of 2004, Pub. L. No. 108-446. Retrieved from www.ed.gov/policy/speced//guid/idea/idea2004.htm

Just, M., & Carpenter, P.A. (1992). A capacity theory of comprehension: Individual differences in working memory. *Psychological Review, 99*, 122-149.

Justice, L. (2006). Evidence based practice response to intervention, and the prevention of reading difficulties. *Language. Speech, and Hearing Services in Schools, 37*, 284-297.

Kauffman, J.M., & Hallahan, D.P. (2005). *Special education: What it is and why we need it.* Boston, MA: Allyn and Bacon.

Kauffman, J.M., Mock, D.R., Tankersley, M., & Landrum, T.J. (2008). Effective service delivery models. In R.J. Morris, & N. Mather (Eds.), *Evidence-based interventions for students with learning and behavioral challenges* (pp. 359-378). Mahwah, NJ: Lawrence Erlbaum Associates.

Kaufman, R. & Wandberg, R. (2010). *Powerful practices for high-performance special educators.* Thousand Oaks, CA: Corwin Press.

Keene, E., & Zimmerman, S. (1997). *Mosaic of thought: Teaching comprehension in a reader's workshop.* Portsmouth, NH: Heinemann.

Kuhn, M.R., & Stahl, S.A. (2003). A review of developmental and remedial practices. *Journal of Educational Psychology, 95*, 3—21.

LaBerge, D., & Sammuels, S.J. (1974). Toward a theory of automatic processing in reading. *Cognitive Psychology, 6*, 293-323.

Lennon, J. E., & Slesinski, C. (1999). Early intervention in reading: Results of a screening and intervention program for kindergarten students. *School Psychology Review, 28*(3), 353–365.

Lerner, J. (2003). *Learning disabilities: Theories, Diagnosis, and teaching strategies.* Boston, MA: Houghton Mifflin Company.

Lunenburg, F.C. (2010). Special education services. *National Forum of Special Education Journal, 21*(1), 1-11.

Martins, B.K., Echert, T.L., Begeny, J.C., Lewandowski, L.J., DiGennaro, F.D., Montarello, S.A., Arbolino, L.A., Reed, D.D., & Fiese, B.H. (2007). Effects of a fluency-building program on the reading performance of low-achieving second and third grade students. *Journal of Behavioral Education, 16*(1), 39-54.

McCown, R., Driscoll, M., & Roop, P.G. (1996). *Educational psychology: A learning-centered approach to classroom practice.* Needham Heights, MA: Allyn & Bacon.

Mesmer, H.A.E. (2010). Textual scaffolds for developing fluency in beginning readers: Accuracy and reading rate in qualitatively leveled and decodable texts. *Literacy Research and Instruction, 49*, 20-39.

Mish, F. C. (Ed.). (1994). *Merriam-Webster's collegiate dictionary* (10th ed.). Springfield, MA: Merriam-Webster.

Moats, L.C. (1991). Conclusion. In A.M. Bains, L.L. Bailet, & L.C. Moats (Eds.), *Written language disorders: Theory into practice* (pp.189-191). Austin, TX: Pro-Ed.

Moats, L.C. (1999). *Teaching reading is rocket science: What expert teachers of reading should know and be able to do.* Paper, American Federation of Teachers, Washington, D.C.

Moats, L.C. (2010). *Speech to print: Language essentials for teachers.* Baltimore, MD: Brookes Publishing Co.

Nagy, W.E., Anderson, R.C., Schommer, M., Scott, J.A., & Stallman, A.C. (1989). Morphological families in the internal lexicon. *Reading Research Quarterly, 24,* 262-282.

Nathan, R.G., & Stanovich, K.E. (1991). The causes and consequences of differences in reading fluency. *Theory into Practice, 30,* 176-184.

National Assessment of Educational Progress (2007). *Reading report card.* U.S. Washington, DC: National Center for Education Statistics. Retrieved from http://nationsreportcard.gov/reading_2007

National Research Center on Learning Disabilities. (2003). *Executive summary of the NRCLD Symposium on Responsiveness to Intervention.* Kansas City, MO: Author.

National Early Literacy Panel (2008). *Developing early literacy: A report of the national early literacy panel. A scientific synthesis of early literacy development and implications for intervention.* Washington, DC: National Institute of Child Health and Human Development, U.S. Department of Education. Retrieved from www.nifl.gov

National Reading Panel (2000). *Teaching children to read: An evidence-based assessment of the scientific research literature on reading and its implications for reading instruction. Report of subgroups.* Washington, DC: National Institute of Child Health and Human Development, U.S. Department of Education. Retrieved from www.nifl.gov

Nunan, D., Griffith, F., & Lee, D.W. (1965). *English grammar and composition.* New York: Harcourt, Brace, and World, Inc.

Palincsar, A.S., & Brown, A.L. (1986). Interactive reading to promote independent learning from text. *The Reading Teacher, 39*(8), 771-777.

Pearce, L.R. & Gayle, R. (2009). Oral reading fluency as a predictor of reading comprehension with American Indian and white elementary students. *School Psychology Review, 38*(3), 419–427.

Polloway, A., & Smith, E.C. (2004). *Language instruction for students with disabilities.* Denver, CO: Love Publishing.

Pressley, M., Allington, R.L., Wharton-McDonald, R., Block, C.,C., & Morrow, L. M. (2001). The nature of first-grade instruction that promotes literacy achievement. In M. Pressley, R.L. Allington, R. Wharton-McDonald, C.C. Block, & L.M. Morrow (Eds.), *Learning to read: Lessons from exemplary first-grade classrooms* (pp. 48-69). New York: Guilford Press.

Rasinski, T.V. (2006). A brief history of reading fluency. In S. Samuels & A. Farstrup (Eds.) *What research has to say about fluency instruction* (pp. 70-93). Newark, DE: International Reading Association.

Rasinski, T., Padak, N.D., & Fawcett, G. (2010). *Teaching young children who find reading difficult (4th edition)*. Boston, MA: Allyn & Bacon.

Reed, D. K. (2008). A synthesis of morphology interventions and effects on reading outcomes for students in grades K-12. *Learning Disabilities Research and Practice, 23*(1), 36–49.

Reutzel, D.R., & Hollingsworth, P.M. (1993). Effects of fluency training on second graders' reading comprehension. *Journal of Educational Research, 86,* 325-331.

Rivera, D.P., & Smith, D.D. (1997). *Teaching students with learning and behavior problems*. Boston, MA: Allyn and Bacon.

Rhee, M. (2011). *Mission statement*. Retrieved from www.StudentsFirst.org.

Roberts, T. A. (2003). Effects of alphabet-letter instruction on young children's word recognition. *Journal of Educational Psychology, 95*(1), 41–51.

Roe, B.D., Smith, S.H., Burns, P.C. (2009). *Teaching reading in today's schools (10th ed.)*. Belmont, CA: Wadsworth Cengage Learning.

Rosenblatt, L.M. (2004). The transactional theory of reading and writing. In R.B. Ruddell & N.J. Unrau (Eds.), *Theoretical models and processes of reading* (pp.1363-1398). Newark, DE: International Reading Association.

Samuels, S.J. (2002). Reading fluency: Its development and assessment. In A.E. Farstrup & S.J. Samuels (Eds.), *Reading researchers in search of common ground* (pp.166-183). Newark, DE: International Reading Association.

Samuels, S.J. (2006). Fluency: Toward a model of reading fluency. In S.J. Samuels & A.E. Farstrup (Eds.), *What research has to say about fluency instruction* (pp. 24—46). Newark, DE: International Reading Association.

Schweitzer, A. (1965). To African tourists. In J.B. Simpson (Ed.) (1997), *Simpson's Contemporary quotations*. New York: Harper-Collins Publishers.

Scruggs, T.E., Mastropieri, M.A., & McDuffie, K.A. (2007). Co-teaching in inclusive classrooms: A metasynthesis of qualitative research. *Exceptional Children, 73*(4), 392-416.

Sendak, M. (1991). On station WAMU, Washington. In J.B. Simpson (Ed.) *(1997), Simpson's contemporary quotations*. New York: Harper-Collins Publishers.

Shanker, J.L., & Cockrum, W.A. (2010). *Locating and correcting reading difficulties* (9th ed.). Boston, MA: Allyn & Bacon.

Siegel, L. S. (2008). Morphological awareness skills of English language learners and children with Dyslexia. *Topics in Language Disorders, 28*(1), 15–27.

Solity, J., Deavers, R., Kerfoot, S., Krane, G., & Cannon, K. (1999). Raising literacy attainments in the early years: The impact of instructional psychology. *Educational Psychology: An International Journal of Experimental Educational Psychology, 19*(4), 373–397.

Spafford, C.A., & Gorsser, G.S. (2005). *Dyslexia and reading difficulties: Research and resource guide for working with all struggling readers.* Boston, MA: Allyn and Bacon.

Steinbeck, J. (1962). Letter to the editor. In J.B. Simpson (Ed.)(1997), *Simpson's contemporary quotations.* New York: Harper-Collins Publishers.

Story, J. (1835). Miscellaneous writings. In L.D. Eigen, & J.P. Siegel (Eds.)(1993), *The Macmillian dictionary of politial quotations.* New York: Macmillian Publishing Company.

Suggate, S.P. (2010). Why what we teach depends on when: Grade and reading intervention modality moderate effect size, *Developmental Psychology, 46*(6), 1556-1579.

Swanson, E.A. (2008). Observing reading instruction for students with learning disabilities: A synthesis. *Learning Disability Quarterly, 31*, 115-133.

Swanson, H.L. (1999). Reading research for students with LD: A meta-analysis of intervention outcomes. *Journal of Learning Disabilities, 32*, 504-532.

Tawny, J.W., & Gast, D.L. (1984). *Single subject research in special education.* Boston: Houghton Mifflin.

Taylor, B., Pearson, P.D., Clark, S., & Walpole, S. (2000). Effective schools and accomplished readers: Lessons about primary-grade reading instruction in low-income schools. *Elementary School Journal, 101,* 121-165.

Temple, C., Martinez, M., & Yokota, J. (2011). *Children's books in children's hands: An introduction to their literature.* Boston, MA: Allyn & Bacon.

The University of Oregon, *Institute for Development of Educational Achievement Website,* (2009). www.uoregon.edu/

Thomas, Dylan (1961). From Texas Quarterly. In J.B. Simpson (Ed.)(1997), *Simpson's contemporary quotations.* New York: Harper Collins Publishers.

U.S. Department of Education Institute of Education Sciences (2010) *Condition of education, children and youth with disabilities report.* Retrieved from http://nces.ed.gov/programs/coe/2010/section1/indicator06.asp

Vaughn, S., Gersten, R., & Chard, D.J. (2000). The underlying message in LD intervention research: Findings from research synthesis. *Exceptional Children, 67*, 99-114.

Vaughn, S. & Linan-Thompson, S. (2003). What is special about special education for students with learning disabilities? *The Journal of Special Education, 37*(3), 140-147.

Volonino, V., & Zigmond, N. (2007). Promoting research-based practices through inclusion? *Theory into Practice, 46*(4), 291-300.

Vygotsky, L.S. (1978). *Mind in society: The development of higher psychological processes.* Cambridge, MA: Harvard University Press.

Vygotsky, L.S. (1981*). The genesis of higher mental functions.* In V.V. Wertsch (Ed.), *The concept of activity in Soviet phsychology.* Armonk, NY: Sharpe.

Wigfield, A., Guthrie, J.T., Tonks, S., & Perencevich, K. (2004). Children's motivation for reading: Domain specificity and instructional influences. *Journal of Educational Research, 97*(6), 299–309.

Zigmond, N., Kloo, A., & Volonino, V. (2009). What, where, and how? Special education in the climate of full inclusion. *Exceptionality, 17,* 189-204.

INDEX

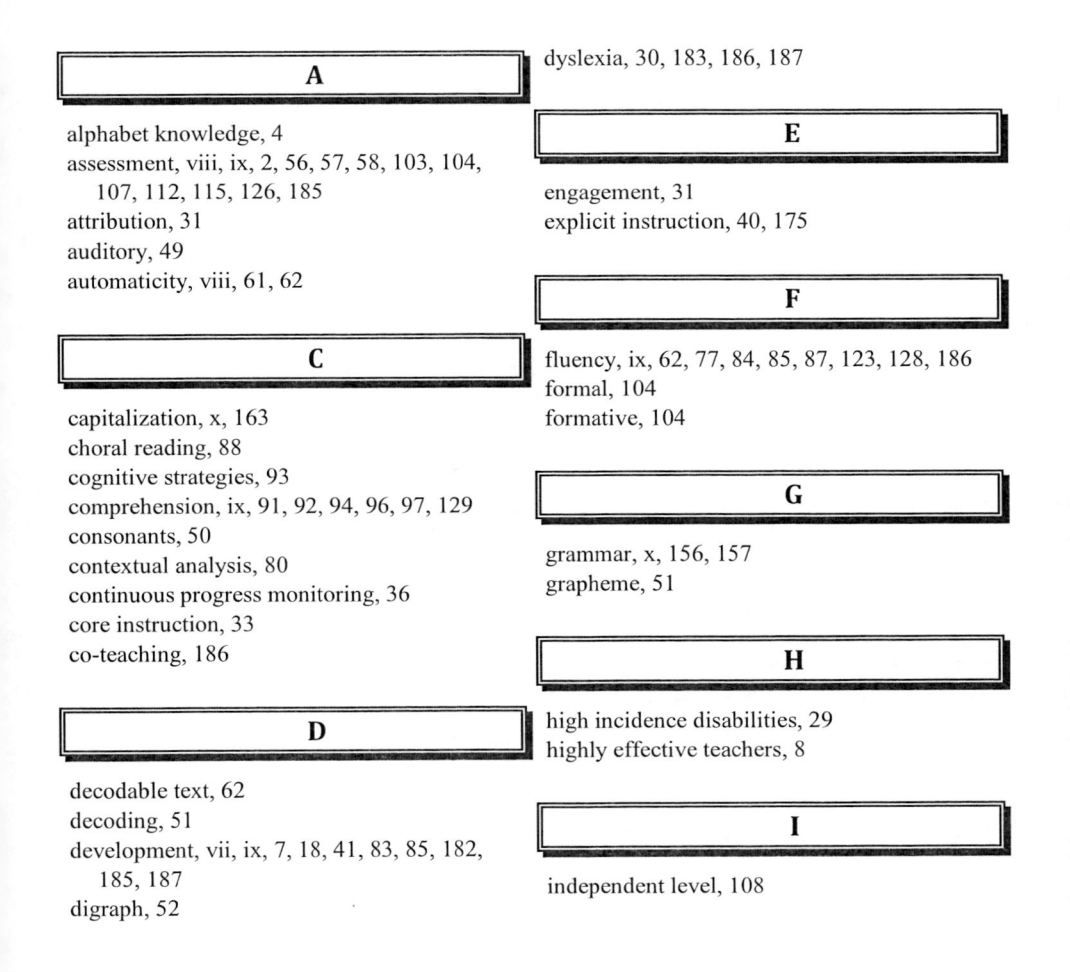